What people are

Ancient F

"Melanie Godfrey shares some of her intimate encounters with Faery and the Elemental Kingdoms. Firstly, she does this through story – each tale born of her experiences with sacred landscape. She goes on to offer valuable techniques, meditations and ceremony to aid the reader in deepening their own relationship with nature beings and the places they inhabit. Melanie's work is heart-felt and deeply personal, encouraging the reader to build their own tales and take their own journey into the enchanted realm of the Otherworld."

Eimear Burke, Chosen Chief of the Order of Bards, Ovates and Druids

"In this book Melanie will lead you into the world of Fayerie that is all around us all the time, but that we so often don't allow ourselves to see and communicate with! It is so lovely to be reminded in such a fresh bright way of the beauty and magic of this world!"

Wendy Andrew, author of *Luna Moon Hare: A Magical Journey with the Goddess*

"*Ancient Fayerie* encourages us to engage more deeply with the beautiful, mysterious, and secret world in which we have come to live. Melanie describes how, through our dreams and visions, we can experience the many races of spirits and energies who inhabit the Otherworlds that run parallel but are intricately entwined with our own. She delightfully and authoritatively tells how we can interact with these spirits by delving into our own psyche, and so the psyche of our world. Through her own experience and processes, she shares how we can expand our own understanding of the multidimensional world in which we have evolved, by interaction with the spirit folk who also share the planet Earth. They are the oldest and the original nature spirits living amongst the most ancient and precious fabric of our world. Melanie's respect for the knowledge she has been shown – and has now passed on – from whom she describes as the Guardians of our world, is tangible and heart-warming. There has never been a more important time to engage with the wisdom to be found in the complex nature of our world. Melanie's passion for this cause, and her contribution to our understanding of how this can be achieved, is considerable and is to be relished in the turn of every page of her wonderful book."

Peter Royston Smith, author of *The Dragon's Edge*

"Melanie's soul feels so pure and ancient and wise to me, and so much is channelled through the space of her words that is profoundly healing and aligning with the very heart of reality. *Ancient Fayerie* brought me home to my soul over and over again with deep breaths, and to curl up with it was to travel to enchanted and wild places with the faerie, Elven, trolls and dragons, to be transported into the very heart of our exquisite and sacred reality upon earth. It is like finding an otherworldly moonstone, shimmering with far colours, and emitting a mysterious song of wisdom and cosmic vision. And remembering that this is the song of who I truly am."

Elen Tompkins, author of *Silver Wheel: The Lost Teachings of the Deerskin Book*

Pagan Portals
Ancient Fayerie

Stories of the Celtic Sidhe and how to connect
to the Otherworldly Realms

Pagan Portals

Ancient Fayerie

Stories of the Celtic Sidhe and how to connect
to the Otherworldly Realms

Melanie Godfrey

MOON
BOOKS

Winchester, UK
Washington, USA

JOHN HUNT PUBLISHING

First published by Moon Books, 2022
Moon Books is an imprint of John Hunt Publishing Ltd., No. 3 East Street, Alresford
Hampshire SO24 9EE, UK
office@jhpbooks.net
www.johnhuntpublishing.com
www.moon-books.net

For distributor details and how to order please visit the 'Ordering' section on our website.

Text copyright: Melanie Godfrey 2021

ISBN: 978 1 78279 477 6
978 1 78279 478 3 (ebook)
Library of Congress Control Number: 2021942470

All rights reserved. Except for brief quotations in critical articles or reviews, no part of this
book may be reproduced in any manner without prior written permission from the publishers.

The rights of Melanie Godfrey as author have been asserted in accordance with the Copyright,
Designs and Patents Act 1988.

A CIP catalogue record for this book is available from the British Library.

Design: Matthew Greenfield

UK: Printed and bound by CPI Group (UK) Ltd, Croydon, CR0 4YY
Printed in North America by CPI GPS partners

We operate a distinctive and ethical publishing philosophy in
all areas of our business, from our global network of authors to
production and worldwide distribution.

Contents

Disclaimer

This book is for entertainment purposes only. The words within this book are from my experiences and personal perspective. This book does not provide any medical advice on physical or mental health difficulties. If you need a medical diagnosis for any physical or psychological conditions, please consult a professional licensed medical practitioner.

For my dear mum, thank you for walking this journey with me.
And for those who wander the earth and believe in starlit Elven magic.

Preface

"Faerie contains many things besides elves and fays, and besides dwarfs, witches, trolls, giants, or dragons, it holds the sea, the sun, the moon, the sky and the earth, and all things that are in it; tree and bird, water and stone, wine and bread, and ourselves, mortal men, when we are enchanted." J.R.R. Tolkien

Imagine a world without ancient stories, without myths and legends. No tales of trolls roaming free on mountain tops, or dragon races in the skies, no fairies dancing on meadows green or water sprites flitting between the bubbles on dancing river tides. I couldn't imagine this. The world would seem still, yet empty of magic; a magic that embodies the mystery of life, an enchantment that inspires my soul to dream of infinite possibilities. Oh, it would be such a dull place if there were no time-honoured tales to tell. My imaginings would seem silly to the few and crazy to most.

But in my imagination, fayeries do exist. Dragons do dance in cloud-filled skies, trolls do hide their treasures of nuts and berries in forest glens, and they walk amid the majestic mountain ranges, their heads almost touching the clouds. Fayeries do hold court and ride tiny white horses with their manes gleaming of rainbow starlight. I'm glad the myths and legends of the earth's cultures were spoken of and retold in stories again and again. I am glad that the elemental kingdoms are alive – in my imagination and vision, anyway. I know many of you feel the same way, too.

There is a place that the spiritual world of fayerie is imagined. My friend, Peter, told me this realm is a place in our mind between wonder and wander – wonder being of the soul; this is where ancient fayerie is envisioned. Yet for many, this part of our mind has been closed over the years, because of being thought wrong or even crazy. Some have completely disregarded this magical world, abandoning it like a haunted house, never to be revisited. I feel this is a shame, for this place between wonder and wander is where our minds access the unseen world of spiritual mysteries. It is a place where our imagination perceives the Otherworld, and where we can build dreams out of stardust for just a moment. Anyone can imagine this majestic land of ancient fayerie. Some envisage it in dreamtime, others in their awakened day. Once these Otherworld's are witnessed, they will never be forgotten.

Fayerie is an age-old name and is a sphere that has always existed. Prehistoric folk were more attuned to the cycles of the year. They interacted daily with the *genius loci,* which is a Latin word, and means the spirit, or guardians of the land. Fayerie is a state of mind rather than a place, it is a realm we enter as we pass through a spiritual dimension into the Otherworld and access higher states of consciousness, this connection can be accessed in our mind through meditation, or through visions.

Animism is a time-honoured belief system, a belief that the trees, the stones, the oceans, the mountains, the weather systems, the animals, and the human beings, all share a parallel feature. They embody a spirit – a soul that gives them life force energy. Animism sees nature as bestowing a language that allows it to subtly communicate with human beings, quite often in profound ways. Animism is about being in relationship with the land. Of pursuing a deeper connection with the earths guardian spirits who will, in turn, gift invaluable insights and share ancient wisdom teachings. The animals, the trees, the stones, have a "voice" that needs to be heard. Animism is an experience that is universal. Enabling humans to re-establish their indigenous natures by perceiving the rivers, mountains, and trees, not just as objects to wield, but as kindred to form a relationship with. The ancient fayerie tales, the myths, and legends of old, all carry elements of animistic understanding.

This book is about deepening our relationship with the land, of visioning beyond our conscious minds. Ultimately remedying a sense of connection and inner peace within ourselves and the wider community, as we remember our natural sense of belonging to the earth. For the Elven ones, the dragons, the gnomes, and the spirit of nature are alive, waiting for us to connect with it in a deeper sense – not just by seeing nature with our eyes, but feeling it with our heart.

The veil between the fayerie and human world is thinning. A few individuals are experiencing fayerie, and supernatural encounters in wild remote places, and sometimes in their homes, too. Yet, there are plenty of people who don't believe in fayeries or that the spirits of a place exist, and others are curious and drawn to seek answers. I choose the latter. I do believe in the world of spirit and the supernatural realms. I trust our ancestors connected with the landscapes, respected the *genius loci*, and made offerings to the guardians of the land, as they sensed a spiritual energy that flowed within the earth.

This book is written in two sections. The first section is about connecting to the heart of ancient fayerie. Where you, too, can explore the landscapes around where you live, and connect to the trees and stones that behold spirit guardians, who await communication with you through your imagination and vision. There is a meditation that will help you to access a higher state of consciousness – the neocortex part of your mind, where the seat of your imagination is. There are tree, stone, and fayerie meditations that will take you on a journey of exploration to find fayerie types who want to guide you in your life.

The second section contains tales from the Celtic Otherworld, stories I created from pilgrimages around Albion's ancient land. These fantasy stories came to me whilst I sat in deep mediative states, where my mind accessed the right hemisphere of my brain and induced deep creative imaginings – and higher forms of inspiration. Where the slightest vision or an image of a dragon in a cliff face or a dryad face etched in the bark of a tree, inspired me to journey in my mind and create stories in my imagination from beyond the veil of rational consciousness, from the world of creative spirit, which we can all access.

Stories sang in my mind, tales of the Elven ones, the People of Peace, who live within the poetic landscapes. I trekked through this wild kingdom, the mountain ranges, the boggy terrain in Scotland, and around bluebell filled Cornish pathways, imagining to myself, which of the many Sidhe, Elven, fayeries, dragons, and trolls, I may meet. Inspiration overflowed. And as the time allowed, I met myself in the wilderness, too.

The whole planet is amassed with Earth guardians, waiting patiently for you to discover, but only if they allow and on their terms. If you ever encounter a fayerie being, embrace a common politeness, and meet them in a ceremonial fashion, as they are not of human mind, so they require a different kind of welcoming. Meet them humbly, and never make promises you cannot keep. Accept that not all the fair folk wish to be discovered, so respect their boundaries and their lands.

The wild places, sacred hills, mounds, and fayerie trees that adorn the Celtic countryside should be refrained from being cut down or destroyed, littered, or nonchalantly walked upon without any kind of respect. And enter fayerie environments with reverence, for the People of Peace prefer to live secluded, secretive lives away from most human eyes, as most humans do not meet the land respectfully.

The People of Peace hid away, and humans forgot who they were. They are hidden, but not in hiding. When you do cross paths with an Elven soul, offer them grace, and show your kindliness. Bless them with a poem, a song, fresh food, fresh milk, bread, cakes, honey, nuts, or mead. Food that you have especially baked will gratefully be accepted, as then they will know you come in warm-hearted and peaceful ways. Be mindful of their boundaries and that you are two different species entirely, even if you have fayerie soul.

When you journey into the Otherworlds, stay impartial, grounded, and calm in nature. Remember to bring your mind firmly back to your human senses, as many folks have been known to become lost in the land of enchantment, it is a timeless place. Not everything is as it seems in their world. Fayerie cannot lie, but they can be tricksters with words and shapeshift. They often wear glamour suits to show themselves, as they are mainly wisps of energy from within the earth and difficult to discern in wild places.

Connecting with the spirit of place has taught me about simplicity, inner peace, and unity. I remembered I am not separate from this wild world we live in, but I am a part of it. Cornwall is my home, and the coastline where I live is filled with enchantment, where mermaid songs echo on the winds, and the rugged cliff-lines are home to endless giants and dragons. The inner landscapes are filled with spritely fayeries and the serious Sidhe beings, whose focus is to bring peace to the world. They are the People of Peace. The fayerie clans are sacred guardians of the earth, and they are there to be appreciated. Embrace these enchanted Otherworlds with the heart of an innocent child – expect the unexpected, and all will be well.

Melanie Godfrey

Section I

The Spirit of the Land

"The miracle is to walk on the green earth, dwelling deeply in the present moment and feeling truly alive."
Thich Nhat Hanh

Deep in the heart of the earth lives the fayerie realm – the unseen world that delights amidst the magical landscapes. The fayeries live amongst nature, and they accompany the animals as they journey through life. As you take pilgrimage through misty woodlands, emerald forests, and pebble beaches, you will encounter flowers, trees, and stones, and every individual species, and rock formation carries their own signature fayerie, and each have a job to take care of the earth. Those who are sensitive may see the fair folk, and these spirits beings show themselves to people they trust – but trust needs to be earned with boundaries and respect.

These guardians of the earth, the Elven, and the Sidhe – also known as the People of Peace – have existed since time immemorial, they are a part of the old ways of spirituality. In the course of time, humans made their domain on earth, and the shining ones disappeared underground into the unseen realms, where only the sensitive or medicine peoples could see them. The Elven knew there would come a time when humans would awaken to their true selves' wisdom, and the Elven one's voices would be heard once more to aid humanity in a healing process – a healing of great disconnection to the earth.

Never underestimate the healing strength of a fayerie, the reliable judgement of a gnome, or the sentimental depths of the mermaids, for they behold the forces of nature within their souls, an intelligence that spans eons.

When a fayerie's work is complete on earth – and this can take thousands of years in some cases, especially for those who embody the mountains, the rocks, and the oceans – they disperse back into the energies of the spiritual realm, merging into the oneness of all that is.

Fayerie are spirit beings that are timid, unseen – so it's best not to expect grand entrances from them when trekking through ivy clad glades. They will appear to you tenderly – only if they choose, and normally when you are off guard.

Fayeries only reveal themselves if they choose too, and one doesn't have to believe in them to feel the subtle spiritual energies of the earth. People who do see apparitions of fayeries, see them as a sparkle or flash of light in the air, a twinkling out of the corner of the eye, or as wisps of subtle energy that leave you questioning if they are real. These sparks of light can be caught on camera as orbs of light. The fair folk can also appear in full glamour suits and enchant with their beauty.

By being present, freeing your mind, and allowing your breath to flow through you, stillness will envelop you. As your mind stills, thoughts from the day will leave you, your consciousness will expand. The essence of stillness within embodies the oneness of all that is in pure consciousness, it is true source flowing through you. By freeing your mind, your own wisdom will arise. In the silence you will hear nature's voice, and the ancient fayerie, through your own awareness. Let your breath flow through you and practise deep breathing every day.

There are different ways to sense the world of spirit and the fayerie races. This is through your unique awareness, intuition, and psychic senses of hearing, feeling, seeing, and touching. Some people have one or two of these senses awakened, or they could be aware of them all. These senses are known as Clair Senses, and they are:

Clairaudience – Clear Hearing – Hearing sounds from the spiritual realm, faint spirit whispers and noises in the inner ear and interpreting these sounds.

Clairsentience – Clear Feeling – Sensing Mother Nature's energy, feeling this energy within our own bodies.

Clairscent – Clear Smelling – Smelling the scent of flowers, or perfumes from a fayerie spirit. If the scent of roses embraces you, and there are no roses nearby, this could be the presence of an ancestor or rose fayerie drawing close.

Clairempathy – Clear Emotion – To empathically tune into the emotional experiences of nature, animals, or places. Clair Empathy is like Clairsentience, where a person feels with their senses the emotions, or energy of a place. Empathic people can tune into the aura of a tree and feel its frequency or pick up on the emotions of the dryad spirit.

Clairtangency – Clear Touching – To receive information through one's hands – information about a stone, a tree, or a flower.

Clairvoyance – Clear Vision – To see with the third eye, by experiencing visions, seeing symbols, or clearly perceiving the fayerie world in their full glamour suits.

Recognising which clair sense is your main strength takes patience, as your sensitivities increase through practicing "intuitive feeling." Intuitive feeling is where you have gut feelings and trust those feelings one hundred percent.

Over time you may find that you sense fayerie beings with clearer vision. One of the main ways of connecting to the Otherworlds is by having a clear mind – a mind that is ready to receive. This will help you to define any messages you are given. Whereby, when in communication with the Elven, fayerie, dryad, gnome, and mermaid spirits you may receive symbolism or images in your unconscious mind, that you can then translate into words in your conscious mind.

The fayerie kingdoms allow us glimpses into their world, glimpses that last mere seconds. They are vibrating on a different energetic level from anything our eyes are used to seeing. We are used to seeing solid structure, not the unseen world. Anyone can connect to the spirit of place and receive information about the subtle spiritual energies that live there; it does not require an extra special talent.

Become open to receiving information and trust the messages you receive from the Otherworld. Not everyone will see nature spirits. Certain folk will feel, others will hear whispers, giggles, laughter, or music. I have heard of people smelling the fragrance of roses, sometimes they smell candy floss, or chocolate, and they sense it is the fayeries close by. People may see flashes of light or sparkles in the air, or a full fayerie manifestation. Refrain from trying to "see" spiritual phenomena if your gift is to "feel," as you will waste your energy. Your individual gift of sensing is what you need to focus on.

Invoke the nature spirits by keeping flowers in your home and leave offerings of pure ingredients. Meditate to connect to these celestial beings. Take walks in the woodlands and notice the wildflowers, the trees and where the moss grows in abundance, now and then the moss carries a luminous glow, and I can sense that the fair folk reside there.

Make your intention clear that you wish to see the fayerie realms. Whenever you think of an individual fayerie you connect to its essence. Sit in silence in your home or in nature and ask them to appear to you. William Butler Yeats, who worked to preserve Irish folklore stories wrote, "for everyone is a visionary, if you scratch him deep enough. But the Celt is a visionary without scratching." Be open to the insights you receive... and have patience.

Fayerie Realms and the Minds Creative Imagination

"The world is full of magic things, patiently waiting for our senses to grow sharper."
William Butler Yeats

I have explained how to interpret the fayerie through your clair sent abilities. Now, I wish to show you how to access the fayerie world through your imagination, through the neocortex part of your brain which houses the seat of your imagination – an area that induces insight and creativity. Great artists, poets and writers would have accessed this part of their brain. Artists such as Paul Nash and the great poets like William Blake, who drew inspiration from the *genius loci*, and produced works of art that inspires us to look beyond – into the Otherworlds.

Those who are not able to intuit fayerie world with their clair senses can use other methods to access the realms of fantasy. By connecting with your inbuilt visualization skills, and your creative imagination will lead you to connect to higher forms of inspiration. But this begins with meditation. Meditation is a doorway that allows you to access the activity of the right hemisphere of the brain, where you "perceive" things that are from your imagination.

Meditation expands your higher state of mind, as it clears your conscious thought. Meditation connects the lower states of the mind, to the higher states of the mind, of creativity, visualization, perception, and love. As your mind becomes still through meditation, you will come into the present moment, and open to the flow of the cosmic forces that will guide you to listen to your heart's council, where you will see the world in an expanded picture, and where your creative channels will open.

As you connect to a meditative state of mind, you can

focus on objects that you encounter, these objects will subtly impact the mind, and project images for you to translate. If the vibrations of the object are natural, your mind will naturally be inspired; nature connects us to our soul's essence. Whatever you touch, the subtle energy within you will connect with, and your intuition translates that meeting for you. For instance, you may be admiring your dog, but your mind will see past the physical body of your dog and into their divine soul essence. You may look at a tree and see beyond its outer image into its subtle energy, or the guardian within it. As you begin to recognize the divine soul essence that is within you, you will recognize that light within others, too. This subtle spiritual energy is within every human, animal, tree, and stone. Meditation is a tool to connect you with your inner light.

People do not have to be psychic to "see" fayeries. My visions of fayerie are often fleeting as, in my opinion, the fair folk do not hang around for long, to be seen. When I see fayeries, they form as wisps of energy, then occasionally shapeshift into full glamour suits, where they adorn beautiful outfits, or even show themselves as rugged troll beings, depending on which area of nature they appear.

Faint outlines of a dragon's image may form in cliff or mountainous regions, and then, whilst in deep meditative states, my mind see's the dragon and creative images then open to the full spectrum of fayerie world, which is a state in-between my imagination and vision. Storytelling flows. Anyone can enter an altered state of consciousness. Some do this by meditating in silence, some use music, or drums to enhance a theta state, whereby the mind deeply relaxes. When in meditation, your subconscious mind will receive information for you to translate from the objects that you see or hold.

Individuals do not have to "see" fayeries or even believe in them to experience the spiritual energies of the earth's landscapes. What is important is that you form a relationship with the land and remember your sense of belonging to the earth as you re-connect to the wilderness, which is a part of your inherent homecoming. This does not involve seeing fayerie; it involves you seeing yourself, interconnected with the world around you.

My friend Peter, and author of *The Dragons Edge*, eloquently expressed to me his view of nature and how he sees the Otherworlds.

"We have a relationship with the Earth. It is a different being in a similar way that your dog is, but we can have a relationship with it based on, as you rightly say, with love – everything starts from there. We start to find ways we can interact with Earth. So, in our relationship with the Earth, we become embedded in the beauty of the natural world around us, and because we are storytellers and need to express ourselves, we give her a persona – a goddess persona. We have, as a species, done this for just about everything – the wind, the rivers, the mountains, and at some point, perhaps we decided it was all so wonderful there must be other humanoid spirits who helped behind the scenes in nature to keep it all going.

So, whether faeries exist or not, the myth has been created and is handed down and told through the generations as an explanation for how the natural world is so mysterious, and her beauty so inexplicable. Our world becomes a tapestry of myth and tales, many of which are so deeply embedded in our psyche that we simply do not question how they got there. When we are in mystical communication with our world, why, how, and for what reason do the faeries and mystical creatures arise. For example, when we are in a bluebell wood or see a headland shaped like a dragon.

In recent history, we have explained everything through scientific explanation. But still the mystery of how it all came to be – the faeries, and dragons, the mystical forces behind our world, beyond the generations of evolution. It is the dragon's dream in the fantasy of *The Dragon's Edge*, and maybe that will take its place in the tapestry of tales we have made for our world. This, if I am honest, is where I have come to with this, because I do not see faeries running around the woods. And as for magic, I have found it merely intensifies the deep feelings of connectedness I feel for my world in an almost overwhelming way."

Meditation to access higher consciousness in this present moment
Basic Meditation technique

This meditation practice can be done on a daily basis. It will improve your wellbeing, and it will also show you how to access your higher state of conscious mind.

Sit in a comfortable position with your back straight.
Place the tip of your tongue on the roof of your mouth, relax your face, and the muscles in your body.
Close your eyes.
Now, use your imagination to forget the external world, let go of external experiences and go further into your mind.
Imagine you are sitting in a quiet place in nature. You feel completely alone. You are at peace and feel safe.
As you slip into this quiet space, your mind may expand. Spend time connecting with the expansive open space in your mind and invite your imagination to awaken.
Gently change your focus to your breath. Feel the air come into your mouth and fill your lungs. The longer you spend doing this, eventually, you will not feel your body but will just sense the breath. Then in your mind, go to another focus point.
Use a mantra or a candle as a focus point.
Use a mantra that you are comfortable with and that is symbolic to you. I use the word Awen which is a word used in Druidry –

Awen is an old Welsh word that signifies "meandering spirit of inspiration" and is pronounced – 'ah-when', or 'ah-oo-e'. I chant this word over and over again, in a mantra fashion, until the flow of inspiration washes over my spirit.

As you repeat a mantra, your mind will rise in consciousness. You will come into the flow of your mind; you will come into a state of thoughtlessness. This place is where you may experience feelings of peace, bliss, and love.

Now, when you have experienced this sense of thoughtlessness and peace, then focus on an object in your mind's eye, such as a stone, a tree, or a landscape. Or even a sparkle of fayerie light that you have witnessed on the landscape.

Invite a fayerie being to join you. And as the spirit being joins you, the stillness in your mind will interpret this being – through your intuition and imagination – and the world that it belongs to.

As you focus on your chosen object, your mind will send your subconscious mind messages to try and interpret.

Your creative abilities and imagination will flow as you reach a state in-between vision and imagination.

With practice, your imagination will interpret the object, and your intuition will try and make sense of it.

This is a place where fayerie tales are created and then put into words.

The Essence of Earth, Air, Fire, and Water

"The earth is what we all have in common."
Wendell Berry

Many years ago, in the 5th century, there lived an ancient Greek philosopher whose name was Empedocles. He came to understand in his dealings with the natural world that matter is made up of four elements. These basic four elements are earth, air, fire, and water. Empedocles believed that all matter on Mother Earth, whether mortal or not, was conscious.

In his study, Empedocles wrote: "Hear first the four roots of all things: shining Zeus (recognized as fire) and life-bringing Hera (recognized as air) and Aidoneus (recognized as earth) and Nestis (recognized as water)." These four elements are the basis of life itself. Each element contains individual energy, holding a unique wisdom. These four elements are not only a part of the earth, but also within our subtle energy bodies.

Human beings are made up of these four elements of earth, air, fire, and water. The earth element represents our material bodies, which consists of various metals and minerals that also reside within the earth. Water is needed to nourish and feed our cells. Fire is required to naturally burn the food which we eat and give our bodies energy. Air is the oxygen we breathe to live.

Finding a balance with the elements of earth, air, fire, and water is necessary, for if we concentrate too much on the element of, say, water, we may become over-emotional, yet if we balance the water element by connecting with the earth element, we invite grounding into our lives. Embracing the air element, we invoke intellect, which will lend our emotions a well-deserved break with rational thinking. And so, it goes.

The planet is the ultimate source of the four elements of earth, air, fire, and water, and these elements behold the great mountains, meandering rivers, enigmatic trees, the weather patterns, the gale force or gently whispering winds. Within the architecture of the mountains and the places in nature are the subtle energies of the fayeries, the Elven, dryads, mermaids, and sylphs. Fayeries dwell in a spiritual dimension, and they take care of the natural material which they most resonate with. These fayerie spirits are a manifestation of energy and enter contrasting realms by shapeshifting. Ancient fayerie serve the planet, living in the 'unseen' realms, yet they can appear whenever they become aware of the thoughts of humans.

As the turning of the seasons takes place, new symbolism in the form of seasonal flowers, trees, and crops, arise. Symbolism is omnipresent and connecting to nature means getting to understand the natural world at a much deeper level. What emotion do specific flowers, trees, or animals, inspire within you? What feelings do they invoke energy-wise? Observe the subtle vibrational essence within all of life.

The energy of earth – The fayerie connected to the earth are the gnomes, dwarves, and dryads. The dryad spirit embodies the essence of the woodlands, and trees. The gnomes work with the stone, mineral, and crystal kingdoms. Gnome energy encourages us to feel grounded, secure, and connected with the earth; they initiate balance. Gnomes gift an energetic strength to our bodies. Mother Earth holds us. Earth energy is communicated with physical effort, by being trustworthy in your actions, and by being respectful in your endeavors. Connecting with the earth grounds me in the present moment. I touch the sacred in everything.

The energy of air – The fayerie related to the air are the sylphs and Imps. Air spirits have a high vibration. The energy of air connects to the mind's intellect, spiritual awareness, and spirit of Awen. Sylphs invoke creativity. Air refreshes the mind – by mingling with the gentle breeze and becoming conscious of each breath. Air energy is expressed in form by having conscious awareness, clarity of thought, ideas, and imaginings. Connecting with air – I transcend into other realms.

The energy of fire – The fayerie identifying with fire are the salamanders and dragons. The spirit of fire is a burning reminder of metamorphosis and renewal, enhancing vitality, warmth, and lifeforce. Fire energy is expressed through courage, enthusiasm, expression, faith, action, and creative flow. Let fire burn away inner stagnation and ignite your spirit. Connecting with fire arouses my kundalini and warms my soul.

The energy of water – The fayerie related to water are the mermaids, mermen, undies, sylphs, and water sprites. Water energy connects us to our emotions, allowing us to express them freely. Water encourages deep emotional cleansing, assisting with release, and teaching us to surrender. The energy of water is felt through our sensitivity, empathy, and, compassionate and forgiving minds. Connecting to water expands my emotional awareness and sense of self-love in the world. I heal my wounded self.

Ancient Fayerie

"Come away, O human child!
To the waters and the wild
With a faery, hand in hand,
For the world's more full of weeping than you can understand."
William Butler Yeats, *The Stolen Child*

In my childhood, I believed in magic, as most children do. As a child I remember going to Anglesey in Wales with my family, we used to visit the beaches and explore the rocks off the coastline. In my mind, I would whisper to the sea creatures, and all of nature. I believe they echoed back. I saw auras around people and in the natural environment. I felt secure in the presence of Mother Earth; nature has always been my companion. From my perspective, energy existed within everything, one that was subtle and ebbed and flowed within the trees, the flowers, the bumble bees, and butterflies. The world, for me, was a place of pure enchantment.

The *genius loci*, or guardians of the land exist throughout the whole world. These custodian spirits originate from the beginning of time. The Elven races are formed of light, a similar energy of light, which is in our interior world, our soul. Certain Elven travelled from faraway star systems and from ancient, advanced civilizations. They spread out across continents, forming individual Elven tribes. All the fayerie existing on Earth are closely related to each other and live in accord with Mother Earth.

The guardian spirits of the land knew there would come a time on Earth where their voices would again be heard, to help humanity remember their relationship with the earth, and the stars. Ancient fayerie is a realm we enter as we access higher states of consciousness, and where the trees, the stones, and all of nature, have an anima.

The spelling of fayerie within this book, instead of fairy, is for me a more antiquated way of referring to these spirit beings who are far from Disney characters and tiny Tinker Bell. Fayerie is a term used by a British folklorist, Katharine Briggs, who refers to these as supernatural beings who wield powers. Fayeries especially flaunt their powers when they shapeshift to adorn flamboyant glamour suits that sometimes omit a spectrum of rainbow colours. They are masters of illusion.

Tuatha De Danann

The Sidhe: "Who are they?" asks William Butler Yeats. "Fallen angels who were not good enough to be saved, nor bad enough to be lost," says the peasantry. "The gods of the earth," says the Book of Armagh. "The pagan gods of Ireland," say the Irish antiquarians, "the Tuatha De Danann, who, when no longer worshipped and fed with offerings, dwindled away in the popular imagination, and now are only a few spans high." *(Fairy and Folk Tales of the Irish Peasantry, 1888, page 1).*

Certain academics believed that the Tuatha De Danann never existed. Their stories are a great mystery, even though many of the early myths and legends spoke about them. Yet, these stories said that they were mythical beings who came from early advanced civilizations, who lost their own lands through an ocean catastrophe, and then went in search of new beginnings travelling on the seven seas to settle on new shores – Ireland being one of these places.

Written within the pages of *Lebor Gabála Érenn*, known in the English language as the 'Book of Invasions', is an anthology of prose whose origins go back to the 7th Century. This book whispers tales about the Tuatha De Danann, claiming they came to Ireland on "flying ships," and ascended in a haze on a Mountain, in County Leitrim. A later narrative says that these "flying ships" were actually sailing ships, but the philosophers translating the anthology may have been trying to justify a nonsensical story, as in the book it reads, "the truth is not known, beneath the sky of stars, whether they were of heaven or earth."

The Tuatha De Danann are a primeval race of beings and were known in the Celtic legends to be the fiercest tribe to ever have settled on Irish soil. But fables tell the tale that they were defeated in a cosmic battle with the Milesians, the Milesians being a tribe, whom scholars believe were the first Gaels in Ireland. After their defeat, the Tuatha De Danann disappeared to the hills, and mountains, to live underground where humans could not find them. The Irish Mythological Cycle, the Ulster Cycle, the Fenian Cycle, and lastly the Historical Cycle echo timeless tales of the Tuatha De Danann. Let us expand our consciousness and embrace our own conclusions about the Tuatha De Danann, of whether they were a race of wise druid people, or supernatural beings who embodied starlight. In my humble opinion, what truly matters is that their stories continue to enchant our souls today.

Fayerie is an old-time word for "all the folk that dwell in the supernatural realms." Sidhe, pronounced Shee, is an old Gaelic word and means fayerie mound. The People of Peace is an expression often used for the Sidhe, as they embody the essence of peace. I refer to the Celtic Sidhe, living within the Celtic landscapes, existing in areas of Ireland, Scotland, and England; "Celtic" is a broad term used. Yet, the Anglo Saxon, Anglo Norman, and Roman cultures greatly influenced many parts of ancient Albion in the last 2,000 years.

The all-wise, Sidhe, rarely show themselves, and to seek them would be futile – unlike the other races of fair folk, who appear more frequently, often fleetingly, seen as sparks of light or clothed in elegant glamour suits. The Sidhe are the ancient kings and queens of old, and one must honour their unseen presence. From my perspective, they originate from the stars, and are the priests and priestesses from the heart of ancient civilizations.

The Tuatha De Danann, or People of the Goddess Danu are said to be the oldest Elven beings, who live in a land of elevated light, called Tir Na nOg. They dwell within Ireland's sacred soil, within the hills and mounds, and the Sidhe knew that parts of the UK held sacred codes and journeyed where their heart beckoned and call it their homeland. Cornwall is known as the land of saints and is sometimes underestimated in terms of the fayerie world. People believe that most of the ancient fayerie went to live in Scotland, but a legion of the Sidhe, and their relatives came to rest in Cornwall, too, in hidden places.

The fair folk went underground, and to expose their abodes is not wise but the earth is in jeopardy and the fayerie are beginning to share their hearts wisdom with human folk. Discernment, and permission should be sought before sharing their stories. One day the Elven ones spoke to me about their sadness for Mother Earth and human's inability to work together harmoniously for the good of themselves and the land, of how mortal folk had forgotten how to have a relationship with the earth. They spoke of a time being upon us, of great change, where balance needs to be restored within the human psyche, but that this would come at a cost of people losing their old ways of "thinking" as they embrace new ways of "being." As the spiritual veil between the two worlds becomes thinner, humans can connect to the *genius loci* with greater ease, and converse with the fayerie realms. The Elven spoke about the ancient fayerie being ready to help humans understand new ways of being in relationship with the land and themselves, a consciousness, where walking the land in honour comes naturally, and of building new communities, where peace reigns, just as it does in the Otherworlds.

The Elven spoke about taking care of the earth and of how people have forgotten how to respect themselves, as "respect for oneself and the Elven ones, follows respect for the earth" they whispered with a smile. People need to remember how to love themselves, and in doing so will show greater care for those around them. Self-love and self-mastery, being aware of oneself and who one is, is key to walking a responsible magical life.

The Elven remind me that all of the land is sacred; no part is forgotten just because humans have disrespected it. There are areas of land that need rewilding and healing, and this can be achieved by bringing parts of nature back to life, especially in built-up areas of land.

For those living in urban areas, the Elven said that those who wish to support the land can start by introducing nature and trees to the communities. Individuals can commune with the landscape, by speaking to the land and holding ceremonies to honour it, and to re-educate those who dishonour it. The Elven told me they do not hold resentment towards people who have made mistakes, they wish for people to learn how to live alongside the land in greater harmony. Certain farming and mining methods have been harsh with the land and this has wounded the nature spirits that live in these areas. Performing ceremonies to apologies and ask for forgiveness to these guardians may help to heal a part of their woundedness.

The ancient fayerie are here to walk by your side, as you evolve, and remember your sense of belonging to the earth.

Good Fayeries and Bad Fayeries

Our ancient ancestors gathered besides the hearthside after the land bade goodnight to the sun and told tales about things that they could not understand, and they were inspired, and invented names for the land, the weather, and the seasons, and the gods, and goddesses, and fayeries of all of nature were born. In bygone days there are tales of fayeries causing destruction and misfortune in people's homes, yet if we look at this now, we can conclude that many folks lived in fear. If their child was born with deformities or illness, it must have been the fayeries that caused these difficulties. If a wife suffered with anxiety or depression, she must have a fayerie attachment; if the milk soured too soon, it must be the fayerie folk; if precious items were lost, the fayeries stole them. And so, it went. Fayeries were blamed for people's ill fate.

William Butler Yeats, author of *Fairy and Folk Tales of the Irish Peasantry,* travelled around Ireland and met with the everyday Irish folk, who shared supernatural stories of sightings of fayeries and mermaids, and many folklore tales were born. These included both good and bad stories about the Otherworld. Yeats said of the folklorists:

"The various collectors of Irish Folk-lore have, from our point of view, one great merit, and from the point of view of others, one great fault. They have made their work literature rather than science and told us of the Irish peasantry rather than of the primitive religion of mankind, or whatever else the folklorists are on the gad after. To be considered scientists, they should have tabulated all their tales in the forms like grocers' bills – item the fairy king, item the queen. Instead of this, they have caught the very voice of the people, the very pulse of life, each giving what was noticed most in his day." (*Fairy and Folk Tales of the Irish Peasantry,* 1888).

Many individuals from the olden days respected the invisible world, yet many of the tales told caused fear in the naive and untravelled folk. The last case of severe abuse that took place to a human being through fear of a fayerie causing trouble, was in Ballyvadlea, County Tipperary, in Ireland, in 1895. It involved a woman whose name was Bridget Cleary. Bridget's soul was thought to have been taken over by a fayerie changeling. This woman endured an illness that had caused her to become frail and changed in personality, not being her usual self. Now, this can happen after a person has had an illness. Yet, at that time, Bridget's husband burned his wife alive, trying to exorcise the fayerie he believed had possessed her. He was later sent to prison for manslaughter, being let off for murder by what the courts termed as "Fayerie Defence."

We need to draw our own conclusions about stories from the past and inspect the demonisation of fayerie kingdom by looking rationally at a person's misfortune. I don't believe a child born with illness or deformity was caused by fayeries, and I don't feel Bridget Cleary was possessed by a fayerie; I believe she suffered cruelty at the hands of her husband. From personal experience, if you respect the spirits of the land, they will respect you. Maybe a lot of the early myths about the fair folk, interpreting them as evil-doers, were spoken about to deter people from disrespecting each other and the land, warning those not to cut down the old trees, disturb hill forts, or build on wild habitats for the sake of development, as this would be met with adversity. The fair folk stories created were blown out of proportion, and as a result, a fear of the fayerie grew. Yet, there are aspects of the Otherworlds we will never understand; the fayeries remain secretive, they are both exquisite and unsightly, enlightened and silly, potent and fragile, and as the thunder-claps and storms rage, the fairies of this world are not all Disneyland; they are powerful energetic forces of nature. They are nature itself. A belief in ancient fayerie entices us to be gentle, and protect the land and, in my opinion, the *genius loci* and great wilderness need respecting greatly.

From personal encounters, not all fayeries are happy to engage with human beings, some are elusive and, we need to respect their wishes by leaving them alone. A minority of the fayerie beings – and this is a small percentage – are still upset with humans for the destruction, and disrespect that has taken place on Mother Earth. Many of them are healing as the land heals. If you ever meet a troubled fayerie, treat them compassionately, and leave them be. Whether or not this small percentage of fayerie souls will ever forgive humans, remains to be seen.

Fayerie Food and Gifts

Each person will work with the fayerie realm uniquely, and some people will embrace accepting fayerie food and gifts, so do what feels right from your intuition. But remember, however alluring the gifts may be, there may be some strings attached. As for food, I do not take food from them either. I gracefully turn down their offerings. With goodwill, the fayeries accept my wishes.

When a fayerie offers a gift through a vision, rather than accept the gift I see it as a symbol of their teachings. For instance, if they offer a drink from a silver chalice, I see this as a metaphorical indication to "drink from the fountain of knowledge," if I am offered a flower, I see this as a sign of what the flower represents. If it is a rose, this symbolises divine love and heart healing.

Language in the fayerie kingdoms is quite different to our world; they do not understand human vocabulary, as such. To say thank you to a fayerie could cause misunderstanding; they prefer you to gift them with something. Entering in communion of thanks with nature is an act of blessing, and to give from your heart is to live in divine union with the natural world. Choose biodegradable gifts, such as honey, bird seed, herbs, rose petals, or a piece of fruit. Sing a song, or play a musical instrument, and you will feel them come alive, enchanted by your melody. And remember, if you ask for a favor from the fayeries, they may ask for one back – choose your communication with the fayerie realms, wisely. The fayeries – also known as fair folk, the other crowd, and the good people, even though they keep their promises – can be tricksters.

Ancient fayerie transports your mind to unlimited depths; they are ageless, and time is of no relevance. Meditations will seem like an eternity with them. So, when returning from a journey, make sure you are fully back in this world and grounded before going about your day.

As you walk outdoors, open your heart to receive messages

from the guardians of the land. These forces of nature shape-shift and appear in many forms and figures. Once you become aware of a few fayerie beings, you will begin to understand that they exist everywhere in nature.

A small word of caution

Sensing subtle spiritual energies of the spirit world is a natural part of who we are, yet many individuals have lost this innate form of intuition. Using our sixth sense has been frowned upon for centuries and deemed an unrighteous thing to do.

It was our early ancestors who walked between the two worlds and accepted psychic sense as a natural state of being. Times have changed and many have lost sight of who they are. Layers of emotional debris cover our innate gifts. To lift the curtain and embrace our gifts may cause fear and unknowing if there is no grounding in self-awareness. Anyone delving into the spiritual arts – be that healing or looking at reopening the third eye and connecting to the Celtic Otherworld – please think carefully before you begin. As you access higher states of consciousness, there may be much buried emotionally within you that may be aroused, uncovered, and brought to the surface, as you begin to open your channels of imagination, and psychic gifts.

If you are feeling unbalanced or mentally unwell, it might be an idea not to meditate with the fayerie realms until you are feeling better. Get to know yourself deeply, so that when you take journeys to meet with the Elven spirits or go on healing journeys to receive insight from your higher selves' wisdom, you will already know yourself and not get lost in the abyss of emotional fallout. Understand yourself first and foremost. It is a magical experience connecting to different states of consciousness through the ancient fayerie. Yet, it is wise not to use these realms as a form of escapism or spiritual bypassing, as no spirit guide or fayerie can replace the knowledge that resides within your own heart's wisdom, which is what you may be seeking.

Guided Meditation to meet with a fayerie guide who wishes to work with you

This meditation will take you on a journey to meet with a fayerie guide who wishes to accompany you on your journey through life. This nature spirit could be a gnome, a dragon, a mermaid, or an Elven spirit. Meet the fayerie realms with an open and loving heart. Journey without expectations and expect the unexpected.

You can do this meditation alone or have someone slowly read it to you.

Firstly, relax yourself, and close your eyes.

Ground yourself by imagining tree roots coming out of your feet and seeing them flow deep into Mother Earth.

Take some deep breaths and, let go of all your thoughts from the day. Feel the power of your breath move through you and bring your mind into the present moment.

Continue to breathe deeply and feel your body go deeper, into a state of relaxation.

See yourself standing at the edge of a pathway.

Begin to walk down this woodland pathway. There are trees on each side of the pathway, and they welcome you as you walk by.

You can hear the birds singing and you feel the sun rays warming your face.

As you saunter further down the pathway, you come across a white hare who is patiently waiting for you. She gazes up at you, her eyes twinkle. You move towards the white hare and bend down to gently stroke her soft fur. She accepts your warm embrace and then ushers you to walk on as she hops by your side.

Further down the pathway, she guides you to a wooden doorway. An oak carved door. The hare signals for you to open the door, so you take the handle and turn it.

Both of you go through the oak doorway and then you come to some time-worn steps. You walk steadily down these steps and onto a stone embankment. You can hear a waterfall in the near distance.

Butterflies flutter past you. Your hare friend ushers you to move forward, towards a flat rock which lays at the edge of the iridescent waterfall pool. She gestures for you to sit down.

You sit on the rock and rest a while. The sound of the waterfall soothes your soul, and you relax, deeper. Peace surrounds this sacred place.

You see bubbles forming and floating up from the foam at the bottom of the waterfall. An enormous bubble floats slowly towards you. As it does so, it gets bigger and bigger; until eventually the bubble is right in front of you. You gaze at the opalescent bubble and notice a fayerie soul within it. The bubble bursts and the fayerie lands gently feet-first on the ground in front of you.

What does the fayerie look like?

Does it have a name? (Trust the first name that is given to you; this may come later in your daily thoughts or dreams.)

Is there any advice they wish to share with you?

Do they have any knowledge about their world to share with you?

Do they come with a symbol, a song, or a poem for you?

Continue sitting by the waterfall, getting to know your new companion. Offer them a rock to sit next to you as you get to know about their life.

Take as long as you need.

(5-10 minutes in silence)

Gently give thanks to your fayerie guide for visiting you and bid them farewell. Slowly get up from the rock you were sitting on. You see your friend the white hare is waiting behind you, she gently hops by your side. You both start walking back the way you came, gently trekking up the steps together and leaving the sound of the waterfall in the distance.

You come to the gate, and the white hare sensitively stands, bowing her head to you. You thank her for accompanying you and walk through the gate back onto the woodland pathway. The birds are still singing their songs as you walk back up the path.

You come to the place where you started your journey.

Gently bring yourself back into the room where you are, move your fingers and toes, feel your body, and open your eyes.

Take time to ground yourself back into the present moment. Have a glass of water, or a cup of tea and a biscuit.

Gentle Grounding Techniques
(If you need extra grounding after meditations)

Connecting to the spirits of nature induces an altered state of consciousness and individuals can become a little ungrounded during and after connecting to these realms. Here is a list of grounding techniques that will assist in bringing you back into the present moment…

Animals – Spend time with animals. Animals are grounded sentient beings that live close to the earth. Being in their presence can bring us down to earth in a gentle way. Stroking animals invokes a sense of peace and calm.

Avoid stimulants – Stimulants can send the nervous system into overdrive, inducing feelings of being ungrounded. These include sugars, refined foods, caffeine, alcohol, and tobacco.

Bach Flower Remedies – Bach Flower Rescue Remedy or Star of Bethlehem Remedy, both remedies have grounding, and calming properties.

Food – Consume grounding foods such as root vegetables, beetroot, carrots, parsnips, turnips, and potatoes. Eat red colored foods, such as berries, strawberries, and tomatoes. Take salts and minerals of the earth like potassium, magnesium, and calcium; these are grounding minerals.

Gardening – Nurture and grow plants; feel the earth between your fingers as you help bring nature to life. As you spend time in the garden you connect deeply with the earth.

Stones and Wood – Hold pieces of wood or carry sea stones, as these will help connect you to the earth, acting as a soothing talisman.

Touch – The human touch can be a grounding and calming experience. If you feel ungrounded, hold a person's hand, have a massage, ask for a hug – this will momentarily help you feel connected.

Walk barefoot – Practice earthing, with your bare feet touching Mother Earth. This is a beneficial grounding technique.

Wash the dishes – This can be a therapeutic and grounding experience.

The Stone Beings

"Stones have been known to move and trees to speak."
William Shakespeare

The stone beings appeared first; they are the most primeval beings. The stone beings will be the last to exist on earth, too. Stones and Crystals hold humanity's ancient codes of wisdom from the beginning of time – until the end of time. In their age-old ways they teach us about transformation, reconnection, belonging, patience, courage, strength, grounding, pristine ways of being, need I say more, they are the timeless teachers of the earth.

William Blake expressed in his prophetic poetry, "All things begin and end in Albion's ancient Druid rocky shores." The British Isles hold exquisite geological treasure. The wee Isle of Iona in Scotland has unique rock formations and is one of the oldest islands on the planet. The subtle energy there is time-honoured. There are certain rocks on Iona that are approximately three billion years old and contain no fossil life within them. A common term for this rock is Lewisian gneiss, and it is composed of many minerals, including feldspar, epidote, and quartz. This rock forms other parts of the Scottish Hebridean Islands, particularly on the Isles of Harris and Lewis. Our ancestors used Lewisian gneiss to build the Callanish Stone Circle on the Isle of Lewis. These are some of the oldest stone beings on the planet.

There are pebbles scattering the stony beaches of Iona, made of white marble with green serpentine, which have been christened "mermaids' tears." Iona marble holds a subtle angelic energy. Scottish marble is also found on the islands of Tiree and Skye, and is from the same geological seam as Iona marble, and consists of bands of white and grey limestone – compressed with green serpentine – created from the chlorophyll of ancient seaweed.

Iona marble is my favourite stone to connect with, as it brings lightness and joy, and creates a balance for the transformational processes within, calming the kundalini energy.

As a child, I would often go to the beach with my nana, as if on a treasure hunt, and we'd both look with affection at the different stones scattered on the shoreline. I used to gift stones to people from an early age, quite unaware of their subtle energetic properties.

Later in life, I began to explore the subtle energies of crystals and stones for healing. I began to work with exotic minerals from all over the world, and these would take me on deep meditations, often to their land of origin. I began to see that although it was exciting to explore different crystals from many continents, I was being drawn away from the beauty of my native land which I eagerly wanted to re-connect with at a deeper level.

I also realised that I had no evidence of where some of the crystals had come from, or whether they had been ethically mined, so I began to focus on the geology of my homeland where, if I borrowed a stone from the beach, I could later take it back. There are some admirable stones that can be found on beaches and walkways, waiting to bestow their ancient energy.

I began to meditate and bond with the stones from the landscapes of the UK. Ancient Albion has treasure stones of agates, blue john fluorite, Cairngorm quartz, Cornish slate, Cornish turquoise, flint stone, Lewisian gneiss, milky and clear quartz, sandstone, serpentine, Scottish marbles, tourmaline, Welsh gold, Whitby jet, and many other semi-precious stones – all carrying energetic healing properties and fayerie allies – especially gnomes, that accompany them.

We are never the owners of precious stone and crystal beings, but we merely show up in a twinkling of a crystal's life and hold them gently for a while. Humans are short-lived in comparison to the crystal's beings, who will go on living long after we have gone. When collecting stones, remember to ask the stone if it is okay to be borrowed for learning, and healing. Certain rocks do not want to leave their homeland and will throw up an energetic protest if picked up. If the stone says a direct yes to being borrowed from the land, then say thank you, and leave a biodegradable offering or a song or prayer, and eventually, return the stone to its place of origin. If the stone says no, however much you love that stone, honour its wishes, and place it back on the land.

When you connect to an area of land, a stone, or a tree, it will become a part of you and that energy will stay with you forever. There is never any need to take stones from the land, for once you have connected with them, their energy will be remembered. For instance, if you have ever visited somewhere as a child, only to later in life forget what that place felt like? To then revisit it by looking at a photograph, it feels like you are physically reliving your time there. Your mind is having a memory and your body is reacting to the experience you previously had.

Connecting to the land you are native to will also reconnect you to your ancestral line. Preseli Bluestone is a stone of the British Isles, it is a stone that brings an ancient remembering to your soul. In the book *Preseli Bluestone: Healing Stone of the Ancestors*, Sue and Simon Lily go on to explain about the healing energy of stones in the passage below.

"Though we have the mechanics for self-healing, we also require the correct raw materials, the energies of the subtle and material world, to maintain a harmonious existence. And harmonious existence only comes when we have become separated from the sources of our physical and spiritual nutrition. "Healing" is not, therefore, an individual act of 'feeling better." It is a realignment of energy and consciousness that allows correct and appropriate nutrition and balance.
Subtle forms of medicine, "energy medicine," do not interact with physical systems or pathways. There seems no apparent

link between working with a crystal or flower and the rebalance or repair of the physical body. But these things can supply us with a link, a connection, a piece of information, that we have somehow lost, and which prevents us from accessing the possibility of an integrated wholeness. Rocks do not heal us, but they can re-orientate our awareness towards a more harmonious relationship with the world.

Standing alone will always ultimately fail. Standing in a state of unified flow will always support life energy." (*Preseli Bluestone: Healing Stone of the Ancestors*, by Sue and Simon Lilly, 2011, page 77).

Meditation to connect to the stone beings

The spirit guardians of the land, exists within all of nature, within the crystals and the stones. This practice can be done in your home or outside, wherever you feel comfortable. Hold a stone from the land that you wish to connect with. When you connect with the energies of a stone or crystal, you may feel the subtle energies of the stone or envision the gnome, or starlit being living within them. For example, you may feel extra grounded; or you may feel a stellar energy of light coming through the rock.

The guardian being within the stone, will teach you about the stone's vibration. They may appear in your mind as a gnome, sharing symbols, colors, words, or songs. Receive whatever appears in your meditation, with an open heart. Trust your intuitive feelings and take all information from your imagination and vision with a pinch of salt.

Hold a stone that is special to you.
Ground yourself by imagining roots coming out of your feet and going deep into Mother Earth.
Take some deep breaths, allow your breath to flow through you.
Bring yourself into the present moment. Let your mind relax and allow your thoughts to come and go.

Now bring your awareness to the stone you are holding.
What does the stone feel like in your hand?
What energy is emanating from the stone?
Does the stone have a gnome spirit who wishes to make a connection with you?
If so, what does the stone being look like?
Ask them why they have come into your life, and what they wish to teach you?
Take your time meditating with the stone, until you feel it is time to put the stone down.
Give gratitude to the stone for communicating with you. Say a prayer or sing to the stone being, or gift it a biodegradable offering.

Ground yourself and come back into the present moment. Take time to practice this exercise with different types of stones...

The Tree Beings

"Trees and stones will teach you that which you can never learn from the masters."
Saint Bernard of Clairvaux

The tree beings came to live on Earth in their own time, far later than the stone beings. These dryad souls have a rich essence to share with humans. The subtle energy within the trees is compassionate and offers insights into our own healing journeys. The spirit of the dryads waits quietly for you to connect with them, and they give with their whole souls, they are forever giving of themselves, and are ever grateful when we give back to them.

There is a pertinent Native American story I'd like to share about the spirits of the earth and the importance of tree beings in healing. In shamanic healing tradition there are three realms, the upper, the middle and the lower realms. The stone and tree beings are a part of the lower realms. Here are some words from the book, *The Shamanic Journey: A Practical Guide to Therapeutic Shamanism*, by Paul Francis, 2017, page 36.

"By contrast, in shamanism, the lower-world is the realm of Mother Earth. It is also the realm of "The People" – Mother Earth's children. As well as us, the Human People, there are the Animal People, the Standing People (the trees), the Plant People, and the Stone People. There is a wonderful native American story that illustrates what the lower-world is about. It goes like this...

The Animal People became furious with the Human People, because of the way the Humans were harming the other People and Mother Earth herself. So, they decided to get together and kill all of the Human People (which they could do easily if they so wished). The Plant People and the Stone People heard about the Animal People's plan. Now, remember, the Plant People and the Stone People are the oldest and wisest of all the People. They have no egos, and so have the most compassion and wisdom, and are closest to Great Spirit. So, the Plant and Stone People called a great council of all the People. At the council, Stone and Plant said to Animal "We do hear you, and we understand your anger towards the Human People. However, what you plan to do to the Humans is not in accordance with Spirit, and as such it is forbidden. The Humans are young and ignorant, and need our teaching and our wisdom. They have also become sick and fallen away from Great Spirit, and need our healing." So, it was decided at the great council of all the Peoples that each and every type of Animal, Plant, and Stone would take on a healing gift. That gift would be given freely to any individual human who asked for it, and each Animal, Plant, and Stone would freely teach any human who asked them for their wisdom. That is in accordance with Great Spirit.

The lower-world is the place where, as humans, we can go to receive both the healing gifts, and the teaching and wisdom from the Animal, Plant, and Stone People, and from Mother Earth herself. It is also home to the Ancestors, the wise humans who live shamanically and in accordance with Great Spirit. The Ancestors keep the shamanic knowledge and wisdom, and so can be our shamanic teachers and guides. The lower-world is a place of love, wisdom and healing. It is as far removed from hell as it is possible to be."

Exploring the subtle energies of the earth, the fayeries of the trees and stones, I visited sacred sites, aged woodlands, and remote beaches. I would sit in the quiet, connect to the *genius loci*, and ask, 'What do you have to teach me today?' Sometimes the lesson of the day would be to still my thoughts and listen to the silence, within the silence.

My mind would wonder into imaginings of by-gone days when our ancestors walked the lands of Great Britain. I would imagine how they ambled through these lands. How would the sea have sung to them? How would the trees have whispered wisdoms to the early priests, the Druids of these Celtic Isles?

I often hold tree branches and tune into their subtle energies. Sometimes a dryad, a tree being, will appear, often gnome or troll-like in appearance, who will offer me insights into their world. Certain twigs or branches I find have fallen from veteran yew trees or noble oaks. The indigenous trees of Albion, the queen beech trees, the protective blackthorn, the gentle willow trees, the alders, the holly, the rowan, the hawthorn, the elder and the elm have individual fayerie allies, and a glorious tale to share, of healing and wise understanding. One could spend a couple of lifetimes getting to know all the species of tree and the teachings they behold. But take your time, as you will be drawn to an individual species of tree that will have much to teach you in this life. They will share their insight and gentleness, if only you become quiet and listen to their tender whispers.

In building a relationship with trees, you are giving back to them, for many trees give of their special energies but do not ever receive anything in return, and they get to feel exhausted. So, next time you visit your favourite tree, build a relationship with it by gifting it herbs, fruit, prayers, songs, or your spoken voice. Talk to them and love them. By recognising and honouring the tree, it will light up in your presence, you will see. Great healing takes place when this happens, because you are transferring your energy of love to the tree. This love amplifies and seeps into the landscapes, and the land transforms.

I once asked an old friend and accomplished druid who now resides in the summer lands, "Where will I learn about Druidry and the Otherworlds? Who can teach me?"

He said:

"You will learn from nature, from the spirit of place, from the subtle energies and guardians of the stones, the sounds and elementals within the wind, the flow and spirit within the water, the animals and how they use their intuition. This is how we connect to our spiritual basis and our ancestors' way. We bring that knowledge into the present moment. We can learn through teachers, books, but our greatest teacher will be nature itself, and our intuition guiding us along the path of life."

Thank you for your wise words, Brian. I followed your words and I looked for the wisdom in nature. I still look today.

Once you begin to reconnect to the land and your inner self, you will find yourself connecting with your own personal dynamism. As I connected to the land that surrounded me, and to the indigenous trees and plants of my region, I saw myself as a part of a great energy system. The trees would offer insights, and after each encounter, I felt altered in a slight way. Trees offer strength, as they are not fazed by anything. They are bountiful in energy and share wisdom if we allow a sensitive connection to take place. If I am feeling emotional, I position myself next to a tree, and my emotion transforms into increased strength and balance.

Lose all expectations when connecting to the spirits of the land and of what fayerie being you think may appear, as they may not appear to be what you thought. For example, I once did a meditation to meet with a tree dryad, holding a piece of rowan tree branch. I expected a dryad to appear that was lofty and thin with a king-size beard, rather like Merlin the wizard. But the dryad that showed himself was a tiny and plump-looking being, no taller than a foot in height. He had a pointy hat and a round tummy, with exceptionally dinky legs. His face was sympathetic but wrinkly and weather-beaten. He carried strength of heart and had an enigmatic character for such a wee soul.

If ten people meditated upon one tree, each person would experience something different. The wise dryad will mirror within us something that may need healing or offer insight for our personal journey. Individuals may experience the image of a fayerie dryad, others may experience colours, feelings, words or music.

Depending on how your felt sense works, take every visual image and feeling with a pinch of salt. These spiritual experiences help you look deeper into yourself and offer answers to the questions you seek. Try not to get fixed on imaginings or visions, but let them come and go, just as the tides rise and fall. Keep a firm boundary of who you are and try not to get lost in spiritual experiences or spiritual bypass your emotional self.

If you have further questions, investigate the parts of you that need healing. The ancient fayerie are like mirrors to help guide you deeper. These spirits of nature help heal the land. They will guide you on how to serve the land – that is, of course, if they choose to. We never command a fayerie, but rather allow their infinite knowledge to wash over us.

Connecting to a Tree Being

To feel a tree's subtle energy:

Go for a walk into a forest, woodland, or park area.

Look around you at the different trees; which one calls to you the most?

Walk over to the tree that lights up, or whispers to you, and sense if it is okay for you to come into its presence. If the answer is yes, gently walk towards it, circling clockwise, then place your hand tenderly on its bark. If the answer in your intuition is no, find another tree which resonates better with your frequency.

As you come into the tree's energy field, either stand with your arms around it, or your back to it, or sit on the ground with your back leaning against it.

Take some deep breaths, feel your breath expand your

consciousness, become aware of the tree against your body. Breathe deeper and say hello to the tree in your mind. Ask the tree if it is okay for you to commune with it. Most tree spirits are happy to "talk" or give energy.

Tree spirits can be a little grumpy if they have just woken up; sometimes they do not wish to communicate and stay sleeping. Patience is key because nature works at a different pace to us.

As you commune with the tree, ask if there is anything it would like you to do for it? Ask if it has any message or advice for you? The energy of the tree spirit may appear in a voice form, or through in a feeling in your tummy. You may get images or one-word answers, like a color – blue, green – or a word – strength, gentleness. You may hear sounds, or music emanate from the tree. These are all messages from your imagination and vision – a gift to enhance your wellbeing.

If you receive a word in your mind saying strength, it could be that the tree's spirit is about strength and is mirroring a quality that already exists within you. If the tree spirit gives you blue, this will subtly encourage you to use this color to heal yourself; the tree is reflecting what you already know within you.

Remember that you are entering into an altered state of consciousness with the tree, so when you come out of the meditation, gently walk away from the tree being and ground yourself by connecting with your body. You may feel different. Renewed, and stronger, having gained insight from the tree spirit. This is the trees sacred gift to you.

To thank the spirit of the tree, kiss it, say a prayer, sing to it, leave a strand of your hair or a tiny bit of seed for passing wild animals or birds. Leave anything biodegradable. Crystals and ribbons are not biodegradable; sometimes ribbon can restrict the growth of a tree if tied to its branch, and greatly disgruntle the dryads. So, think twice before tying ribbon around branches, however well-meaning this may be.

Awakening the Sacred Heart of Fayerie

"There is a place in you that is the eternal place within you. The more we visit there, the more we are touched and fused with the limitless kindness and affection of the divine. If we can inhabit the reflex of divine presence, then compassion will flow naturally from us."
John O'Donohue

Imagine yourself laying beneath a starry-filled night sky. The moon is full, with an array of shooting stars dancing around it; it is just you and the universe. As you gaze at the twinkling sky, imagine your heart expand in a moment of awe. The feeling you have is intense and explosive. In moments like this, the heart awakens, and you truly connect to your sacred heart space, you awaken the sacred heart of fayerie within you.

The fayerie kingdoms are a part of spirit world and live from a heart space of limitless awe and wonder. They are divine beings filled with compassion and knowing, they are nature itself. When you open your heart space, you become a mirror to the Otherworlds, enabling your communion with ease and grace. As your heart fills with joy and lightness, you will sense the spritely realms of the Elven tribes, of mermaids, dragons, gnomes and water sprites, trolls – all the fayerie races.

It is the heart that receives divine messages, not the intellect. And although it is imperative to use our critical thinking and not lose our mind's ability to interpret wisdoms as we connect to the compassionate side of ourselves, put the intellect aside when receiving divine messages. Sensing the fayerie realms come from an intuitive feeling sense and is a natural part of our human experience. The felt sense is not something that happens outside of us, it is an internal feeling where our mind processes and interprets the world around us.

The heart is a portal of intuition. In becoming heart-centered, you walk a path of being in your truth. The fayerie races are truthful beings, they never lie and are bound by a primordial language that once made, promises must be kept. The heart is where you will discern your truth, and not give promises you cannot keep. Tuning into spiritual dimensions requires you to feel from your heart. Love conquers fear, reflects anger, calms conflict, and dissipates negative energy. Love is a powerful frequency in the universe, and the fayerie world resonates with this higher vibration.

Lightheartedness encourage fayerie communication. In the shamanic communities around the world, shamans working for spirit world have a sense of humor because they know that having a laugh is the quickest way to get into their heart space. Becoming playful, and initiating humor in your daily life, will raise your energy so that higher energies can engage. If the atmosphere is dull, and depressed, the vibration will lessen, and the spiritual energies will find it difficult to connect. The fayerie realms resonate with a humorous spirit. Elven souls exist in their heart space.

The act of true listening is a skill. By actively listening, you are putting your own thoughts aside and giving your time to another. Listening takes observation and stillness. True listening will not only nurture your relationships it will also help your communication on a clairaudient level with the Elven worlds.

Honor any information that you receive from your felt senses – of feeling, hearing, or seeing – and accept information that comes your way. Try not to discredit your abilities or think that your interpretation is not as promising as the next person's just because you feel spirit world but do not hear or see them. Trust the information you receive as this is special knowledge for you from the Otherworld.

Exercise to connect to your heart's essence

Place your hand or hands over your heart and breathe into this space. In this present moment, feel your gentle heartbeat pulsate, breathe into that heartbeat, and recognize it as the same rhythm as Mother Earth. Expand your heart energies, visualizing a pink light emanating from your heart space. Send this pink light through and around your body and then down into the earth, so that your whole being is surrounded by a loving energy field. If you feel yourself going back to your mind and logic, gently bring your focus and feelings back into your heart space once more.

With your hand still resting on your heart, sense what it feels like to rest in your heart space. Your heart center is a place of peace, where you receive moments of divine contemplation. Whatever is happening in the world, let your mind rest. "Feel" into this heart space often, so that eventually you will be living from your heart in all you do. Do remember to critically think, as you will need this for balance in your life.

The more heart-centered you become; your sensitivities will increase. As you fine tune your "feeling" sense, you will perceive the spiritual realms with greater ease. Ancient fayerie is more a state of being, than a place. It is an embodied connection with the earth.

Fayerie Code of Ethics

"Integrity has no need for rules."
Albert Camus

Knowing the earth heals herself, in her time-honored fashion. I often contemplate how I can be of service to the earth without overwhelming myself with the complexity of the environmental issues that are taking place. So, I took charge of my own environment and healing journey and simplified my life as much as possible.

In seeking a harmonious existence with life, we can learn to live in balance with the natural landscape that surrounds us. It is said that, in the beginning, humans came from the sea, and we will probably return to it one day. We have the same heartbeat as the earth.

It takes time to heal our trauma-based consciousness to live from a heart-based consciousness. In healing ourselves and taking responsibility for our actions, we learn to live in congruence alongside the wild forces of nature, and appreciate the guardians of the land.

On a practical level, we can help the earth and respect the fayeries in several ways:

- Be discerning in all you do.
- Be of service to the earth. Give back to the trees, the flowers, and all of nature. They give so much and become exhausted by giving and giving. Honour them by giving back. Do this in the form of friendship, song, prayer, offerings, and your love (the voice, using tones, prayers or song are powerful vibrations of love and healing).
- Believe in fayerie, as in my thoughts, they do exist – just in a different dimension, and they are not always seen

with the human eye. By being acknowledged, the spiritual world of fayerie expands in energy, and connection to them grows.

- Believe in magic. Oh yes, this is a fayerie strict code.
- Drive less and use fuel efficient cars. Use public transport, cycle, or walk.
- Eat less meat; or try vegetarian or vegan food.
- Fayerie tales. Before you share stories of your encounters with the Otherworlds, ask for the fayeries blessing before you do so. Not every tale is meant to be told.
- Have faith in the great mystery.
- Keep your word. If you make a promise to the fayerie world, be consistent, and keep their faith.
- Kindle your inner voice, and individual calling – cultivate what feeds your soul – it is the key to your freedom.
- Leave bio-degradable offerings in ceremony and to give thanks – such as fruit, nuts, seeds, bread, honey, milk, or mead. Or prayers and song are always welcomed, too. Bear in mind that chocolate is not always an appropriate offering to leave outdoors for the fayeries. Although fayerie like sweet gifts, the chocolate may be consumed by the wild animals and can be toxic. Consuming food once it has been offered to the fayerie realm, is not a wise decision, as the essence of the food will be taken and therefore may not energetically resonate with human bodies. Likewise, when being offered fayerie food from the other realms, remember that it may take you to another dimension, or may not suit your energetic body.
- Live in harmony with your environment by taking only what you need and give back to the earth if you do take any flowers, herbs, stones.
- Musical inspiration. Fayeries love music, so play your flute or sing a song to them and honor them this way.
- Pick up litter wherever you go.

- Plant more trees and wildflowers.
- Practice compassion to all the living creatures, be that human, horse, dog, cat, ladybirds, butterflies, the trees, and flowers, and to yourself – as we are all interconnected.
- Reduce waste, reuse materials, and support local charity shops by donating unwanted goods.
- Respect the fair folk's privacy. If you pass by a fayerie court, or you witness them at council meetings. Look away and leave them be. Certain things that the fair folk do are private.
- Support organizations that protect the woodlands and wildlife, such as The Woodland Trust, and local wildlife charities.
- Use earth-friendly household cleaners and body products.
- Walk a heart-centered path.
- When taking pilgrimage in nature, tread gently on the land, and honor the *genius loci*.

Sacred Ceremony for the Ancient Fayerie

"The clearest way into the Universe is through a forest wilderness."
John Muir

Since time immemorial, humans honored their connection to the earth, by giving thanks through prayer. The reason for holding ceremony is to celebrate the life-giving energies of the landscapes, the guardians of the land, the ancestors, and the living essence that flows around us in a perpetual manner. We connect to the spiritual part of ourselves when rituals are created; we rewild our soul to the subtle energy that surrounds the earth, readdressing equilibrium, harmony, and peace.

Ceremonies can be as simple as lighting a candle, and sitting in quiet contemplation, giving gratitude to your intended source, or ceremonies can include sacred instruments, music, chanting, costumes, and offerings. It is a time for humans to rediscover their sacred belonging to the world around them, and a time to connect deeper to the *genius loci*.

As the planet goes through her own transformation, humans will also transform, and the fayerie are here to support this transition with their guiding wisdoms. They are here to counsel us in times of need. If only we open our hearts and listen.

What better way to honor the spirit of place than by creating a quiet moment to show gratitude? Healing can be offered to the guardians of the land, as they are constantly giving. Focus healing light on the plants, the trees, the flowers, or anything that calls to you. The fayeries, and Elven, share their healing light with us each day. In exchange, we too can invoke source light into our own bodies and send this energy out from our hearts through our hands, to the trees, plants, stones, and crystals.

The stones and crystals we are caretakers of may be wounded from the mining sources they came from. They may not have wanted to leave their land of origin. Although it may be impossible to take a crystal back to its source in Brazil if you live in the UK, you may ease the woundedness of the crystal by performing a forgiveness ceremony and apologize to the stone being.

Ceremony is about being in service. But before you create a ritual, make sure that you are grounded. This can be done in numerous ways. I visualize roots growing out of my feet and I see these roots going deep into the middle of the earth. Then I imagine the Earth's healing energy rise to meet me.

Prepare in advance for your ceremony. Guidelines on creating ceremonies are useful, but no-one can teach you about the essence of ritual; you must feel into your heart and allow them to flow. Think about ways you can be of service to others, the earth, and the Elven. Create your own rituals that heal the earths guardians and the animals upon her.

To begin, clear and heal your space with a prayer or a blessing by burning herbs such as juniper, lavender, mugwort, meadowsweet, rowan or yarrow using an old method of "saining," which has its roots in the Scottish culture. Then create a circle with a special wand or imagine a bubble of light surrounding you that only allows the highest energetic light to enter. Many cultures, including the neo druid traditions, invite the elements of earth, air, fire, water, and spirit to help create their sacred space. By working together, your energies merge and transform the environment.

Ask the guardians of the land to witness your work. Invite the ancient fayerie, the Elven and the ancestors to join your ceremony days or even weeks before it takes place. That way they will await your presence on the day.

Ceremony is about honoring the land and enjoying your time doing so. Let your imagination flow when creating sacred ceremonies to connect to the individual fayerie races. Celebrate the dragons, the Elven, the merfolk, the stone beings, and the tree beings.

Creating Ceremony with the elements of Earth, Air, Fire, and Water

Use your imagination to create a ceremony with the element of earth, air, fire or water to help encourage change in your life or heal aspects of the land.

The element of earth – the dwarves, the gnomes, the troll beings are there to assist in shadow work and will help remove negative emotional patterns in your life. Call on the energy of the earth spirits in ceremony to help heal aspects of your shadow selves. The earth dwellers assist in clearing layers of discord and disharmony deep within the earth.

The element of air – the sylphs help to clear your mind of negative thoughts, bringing clarity and creative life force energy through your breath. Call on the energy of the air spirits in ceremony to help cleanse your intellectual mind and breathe life into new ideas. The air spirits help clear negative energy from sky pollution.

The element of fire – the dragons bring the aspect of fire for transformation, which burn away energies within you that you no longer need. Call upon the energy of dragons when in ceremony to invoke renewal, as the sacred fires will burn off old ways of thinking and lift your consciousness. The fire spirits transmute negative energy that has built up over large areas of land – land that has been oppressed.

The element of water – the merfolk helps to wash away emotions that are not serving you. Call on the energy of the mermaids in a ritual to help you explore your emotional self and release any stuck emotions. The water spirits help to clear the energetic imprint of ill-treatment within the oceans.

Ceremony to honor the Ancient Fayerie

1. Invite the guardians of the land to join in your ceremony. This can be done minutes, days, or weeks in advance.

2. Gather your tools for the ceremony. Then set intention, (this ceremony will be to honour and give gratitude to the ancient fayerie).

3. Find a special place to hold the ceremony, in your home or nature.

4. Ground and center yourself in whichever way feels most comfortable to you. Earth yourself by imagining roots coming out from the bottom of your feet and flowing into the earth. Take some deep breaths and come into the present moment.

5. Place your sacred tools and offerings of a biodegradable nature into the middle of the ceremonial space. Draw an invisible circle around you three times; this can be done with a special wand you possess, or with your finger. Start wherever you wish, but traditionally this would be in the east, invite in the elements of the air, from the east; fire, from the south; water, from the west; earth, from the north; and spirit, from up above to join, enhance, and protect your sacred space.

6. Once you feel comfortable in the ceremonial circle, speak your intention. (I come with a peaceful heart, I give gratitude to the land, my ancestors and the ancient fayerie that have joined this sacred ceremony. I honor my connection to the ancient fayerie who live alongside the earth).

7. Invite source light, or the violet flame into your body, and send this light out through your heart or your hands to the trees, the stones, the animals, the Elven, the fayerie and all their relatives, and the whole world.

8. Invite a fayerie soul to communicate with you, listen to the message they carry.

9. Offer gifts and give gratitude. Offerings such as – feathers or milk, mead, fresh baked bread, apples, or nuts. Offerings from the heart. Make sure your offerings will not cause harm to the wild animals (like chocolate) if they consume it later.

10. Sit for a while longer resting in your heart space, contemplate inner peace.

11. As the sacred ceremony comes to an end, close the space by drawing a circle in an anti-clockwise direction, three times. Start wherever you wish, but traditionally in the north.

12. Give thanks to the guardians of the land, the ancient fayerie, and great spirt.

13. Place the offerings of an edible nature, near the base of a tree for the wild animals to eat.

Ceremony of forgiveness for the stone beings

A forgiveness ceremony can be performed with any creature, tree, or stone being. Much of the natural environment has been hurt at the hands of humans, and the nature spirits appreciate any human folk who recognizing this and understand the earths suffering. Then healing begins. Certain stones are sad about being mined and taken from their land of origin. Perform small ceremonies to apologize to the stone beings. Keep these ceremonies simple:

Seek a special place in nature or your home.

Centre your being, in whichever way feels most comfortable for you. Connect to the earth by imagining roots coming out of your feet and flowing into Mother Earth.

Breathe deeply and let go of thoughts from your day.

Light a candle for this ceremony if you feel called to do so.

Set an intention to apologies to the stone being if they have been harshly mined, by putting miners at risk and destroying the land.

Hold the stone close to your heart, and counsel it. Bring source energy into your body. Send this light out through your heart or hands to the stone. Inform the crystal that you will honor and will take care of it. Or place the crystal back in the ground from where it came from, as this is the greatest healing you can offer it. Give the stone being, the gnome it belongs to, time to grieve or speak. Hold space for the stone being as their energy transforms.

As the ceremony draws to a close, whisper words of thanks to the ancient ones.

Gift an offering to the stone being.

Put out the candle flame.

Sacred Sites

"Your sacred space is where you can find yourself again and again."
Joseph Campbell

As I became aware of the spiritual and telluric energies of the land, it not only gave me insights about the Elven, and the guardians of the land, but it also connected me to the life force energy within myself. I visited sacred sites around the Isle of Albion that rekindled a flame within me, an inner knowing, and a re-connection to all that exists, a connection our ancient ancestors would have understood.

The Celtic landscapes lit up the animist within me, and I no longer felt disconnected to the earth but recognised that I am a part of the natural world. For the second time in my life – the first being when I was a child – I started listening to my heart, which is the centre of the soul. I connected to my innocence and intuition. I felt drawn to visit sacred places in the British Isles, Ireland, and the Orkney Islands, thin places like Glastonbury, the Hill of Tara, Iona, Newgrange, the Ring of Brodgar and holy wells and ancient churches in Cornwall, which is known as the land of saints. These ancient megalith sites behold the *genius loci* – the spirit of place, and they carry energies from sacred ceremonies, which were held by the ancient Britons who lived, worked, and danced around the cycles of the year.

Our ancestors respected the cycles of the year. They honoured the sun and the moon and lived in greater harmony with the land. At these ancient sites, I cried tears of remembrance, of a lost inner knowing – something my soul had been yearning for, yet I was unsure what it needed. During this time of searching, I felt a resurrection of my Celtic soul, my DNA sang on the Celtic landscapes from where I had lived and died countless times.

The whole earth is sacred. But there are some places that feel extra special due to the telluric energy, and underground water systems they hold. Nature spirits gather at the sacred sites of the world, and these sites are often portals to the fayerie realms. I often wonder if the visions I have are made up by my intricate imagination. Sometimes, I know they are, yet in some instances there are too many coincidences and I've had to doubt they are not just my imaginings but something more that I cannot make sense of. One incident was when I was sitting in Chalice Well gardens in Glastonbury, it is always peaceful there. As I meditated upon the subtle energies at the main well, I was shown a vision of a stunning luminescent angel who was accompanied by an ivory unicorn.

I sensed they were companions, and I felt immense peace thinking about them both; bubbles of divine energy rippled through my body. I gently came out of this meditation and wondered if my vision had been true. If not, how blessed was I to imagine such radiant beings? Later that afternoon, I walked into the Chalice Well shop. While I stood talking to the shop assistant, I noticed a painting behind her. It was an image of the Chalice Well angel and unicorn – the exact same image that had been shown to me earlier in the vision at the well. I felt awestruck.

It came to my awareness that different people experience similar spiritual imprints at the same place. In certain instances, it is useful to share our spiritual experiences with like-minded souls and appreciate our individual experiences. Are these spiritual visions coincidences, imaginings, or real? I think, at the end of the day, we may never know the full truth, however much we search for evidential truth about spiritual phenomena, and the fayerie realms. There is no proven evidence that the Otherworld's exist, apart from what we 'see' within in our minds eye. And we might drive ourselves mad in the process, of trying to find the truth. The great mystery is, after all, immeasurable and the further we travel, we may conclude, the less we truly know. So, let visions and experiences come and go as ripples on a stream.

As we embark on pilgrimage, seeking sacred sites and the spiritual essence that reside at these powerful nemetons, can be life-changing, the energy at these sites imprints on our energy systems, and we are charged up, like solar batteries. In my experience, visiting ancient sites has left me feeling profoundly and energetically changed by the powerful energies of the place. Ancient peoples could see and feel energy at a much deeper level than we do today, as they were not consumed by modern day technologies that dull the senses. I feel many of us have forgotten how to live simply and feel into the secrets of the land.

Ancient people knew about earth energy lines – an underground phenomenon, which can also be experienced over water and in the air above. Our ancestors may have sought out powerful telluric energy points on the land to build their temples and stone circles, making sure they were in alignment with specific star constellations. Most churches are built on time-honored sites, which ancient settlements may have used as a base for sacred worship or even sacrifice. Either way, the energy at these points is often powerful and potent, in my experience.

Christians built their temples on sacred land that had previously been used by pagan communities. Often the altar points or font area in a church has a strong energetic pulse where a crossing-over of ley lines occurs, and if you have dowsing rods, you will sense this crossing of energy lines. I love visiting some of the older churches, as I can feel the primordial energy that they have been built on and where new Christianized energies of worship and ceremony take place.

In 1921, archeologist Alfred Watkins proposed his theory of ancient pathways, indicating that ancient sites were connected in straight lines. Alfred's theory was that these ancient lines that fell across our countryside and land were noticeable by the megaliths that marked them and were also detectable by dowsing to check the marked track line. Alfred Watkins states in his book, *Early British Trackways*, that:

> "primitive people with few or no enclosures used the shortest distance to access places in the form of a straight line and were given sighting points. These sighting points were either constructed of earth (in the form of mounds, hills, or mountains), stones, water, or sometimes trees. Sacred wells were sometimes a terminal in the line, and often included as secondary points."

These ley lines cross all over the world, connecting sacred sites in straight lines. Ancient people must have walked these lines on pilgrimages or to sell their goods. Many of the ancient Neolithic megalith, such as Stonehenge, the Standing Stones of Stenness, and the Ring of Brodgar, are all built on old trackways. Alfred also states that:

> "churches, if ancient, seem to be invariably on (not merely alongside) a ley line, and in many cases are at the crossing of two leys. This put the siting point to a new use. In other cases, a mark stone (ancient megalith stone) became a church site and the churchyard cross."

According to ancient folklore, fayeries have been known to use ley lines, taking a straight route between sacred sites of significance, where their homes and portals reside. The straight leys that adjoin fayerie paths and forts to certain mountains and sacred springs were sometimes known as "spirit paths" and were of use to the fair folk as they travelled the land. They are probably still used by them today.

However, we must not confuse ley lines with telluric energy lines, as they are both unique. The telluric energy lines are of a subtle energetic nature and run through the earth like a meridian system, weaving across the landscapes as a snake would, much different to the straight ancient pathways. The ancient fayerie understands this, and they resonate with both the earth energy lines and the ancient trackways. Places of power, such as standing stones and megalithic sites, can sit on both the ley lines and earth energy lines; these sites are often portals to the Otherworld and alignment points to specific star systems.

Our ancient ancestors connected heaven to earth at hallowed places. They believed that the souls of humans entered through a still point in the great spheres, and they also exited at star constellation points, as their soul transitioned at the time of their passing. The Isle of Tintagel Castle rests below the Great Bear Star – Ursa Major, which points directly to Polaris, the North Star. This ancient island is a place of sacred worship and ancient kingship initiations.

In Cornwall there are many stories of pixies, mermaids, giants, and fayeries, and of saints bringing miracles to everyday folk, and legends of King Arthur and his most trusted advisor, Merlin the enchanter, and prophet. Merlin's cave lays directly underneath what was once known as the Great Hall of Tintagel Castle. The cave once housed sparkling milky quartz crystals, regarded as the White Tintagel Crystal or Merlin's Stone, and there are gnostic secrets within this broad cavern. Cornwall is famous for misty coastlines with tales of pirates hiding treasure on its shorelines. But as sea mist envelopes the land at Tintagel, it is extra mysterious, and many wild imaginings take place – imaginings of Merlin and Arthur meeting to discuss matters of distinct importance – imaginings of our ancient ancestors taking shamanic bear initiations within the mysterious cave. Merlin's Cave connects to the essence of Marzhin Gwyls and is a place of pure fayerie magic.

Glynn Nathan, which is Cornish for St Nectan's Glen – is another thin place in Cornwall. It is a timeless fayerie dwelling, that has rejuvenating waterfalls filled with healing waters that replenish the weary traveller's soul. It is a place where our souls are revealed and we are shown our true selves wisdom, if we care to look deeper. It is a place where a sacred twin, earth energy line named Merlin resides. There are tales from St Nectan's that I keep close to my heart. You must feel the charm that this sacred site holds for yourself as you connect to the *genius loci* and await possibilities.

When visiting sacred sites, stone circles, quoits, wells, and forts, you may find people performing ceremony at them, honoring the ancestors and guardian spirits, that live in the place. In turn, the guardians honor them back. We do not know for sure what stone circles or megaliths were used for. It is a mystery, but there is a strong indication they were used for sacred ceremony, as astrological location points, for teaching the healing arts, for healing the sick, as burial places of kings and queens, as initiation places for priests and priestesses, or as a meeting place to commune and honor the spirits of their time.

Archeologists in Orkney have uncovered Neolithic settlement sites and a group of buildings in the Ness of Brodgar and barn house areas. There have been hearths discovered at the entrance to a few of the houses, and a person would have had to cross hot embers or smoke in the hearth to enter these houses, indicating some form of cleansing ritual before entering these sacred spaces. These unusual buildings are unlike other houses uncovered and did not have domestic tools within them. It is evident that these houses were used for ceremonial purposes. The Ring of Brodgar stone circle and the Standing Stones of Stenness are situated a little walk away from these unearthed buildings. The ancient stone circles on Orkney were said to be the epicenter of worship for people in the British Isles in the Neolithic time, and the energy at these areas is potent, powerful, and full of inspiration.

The strong frequencies at stone circles are apparent through the feelings you receive whilst in their vicinity, feelings of profound peace, and bliss. Circles formed in a ritual setting offer an extraordinarily protective energy and being inside a circle creates space for meditations, journeying, ceremony, and entering the Otherworld to meet the ancient fayerie. Circles of high stone megaliths also offer a perfect place for encompassing sound and acoustic vibrations which could possibly have enhanced any ceremonial music of the ancient peoples to enter trance-like states for Otherworldly journeys. When I stood in the center of the Standing Stones of Stenness on Orkney, I clapped my hands at a certain point in the center of the stone circle, and the clap echoed like being in a cave. It was quite extraordinary.

The ancient Druids would gather to perform sacred ritual, to commune with the spirit world and connect with the star constellations in sacred groves in the woodlands. The trees would have formed a circle, outlining the grove. Circles and trees hold distinctive energies.

Thin places are land where heaven and earth are said to be only three feet apart. It is believed that the phenomenon of the veils being thin on the sacred Isle of Iona can possibly be attributed to the fact that the island is mainly composed of quartz, which vibrates at a high frequency, but also to the fact that the south end of the island adorns one of the oldest rock formations on the planet. These primordial stone beings are recorded to be approximately three billion years old, a Lewisian gneiss that has no fossil life found in it and releases above-average levels of radiation.

It has been documented that areas of land which discharge greater levels of radiation – such as at Sancreed Holy Well in Cornwall – the veils are thinner, and spirit activity and psychic phenomena occur more frequently, and many fayerie souls frequent Sancreed. This could also add to the mystery that is Iona. Once known as Druid Isle, it is an island inhabited with wise Elven, primordial dragons, and classical mermaids. I imagine the ancient Celts and their priests would have recognized the prominent *genius loci* on Iona and built their druid school there for that purpose. Iona has been a pilgrimage site for centuries, and after the time of the druids when St Columba arrived, it became an early Christian settlement site. Colum Cille arrived from Ireland in 563AD and built a monastic community – the ancient sanctity that is Iona. Kings from far and wide were bought there for burial, for it to be their final resting place. Today, people from all over the world pilgrimage to Iona to experience its unique sacredness.

For a moment, think about the geological structure of the land you are living on. In Cornwall, there is mainly slate, granite, and quartz, which emits a strong steady energy. In Scotland, much of the earth is volcanic in structure. At Stonehenge, the earth is chalk-based, with some of the megalith stones being sarsen, which is from Wiltshire, and Preseli bluestone, which is from Wales. In the surrounding area of Salisbury Plain, it is chalk-based, with Avebury stone circle being sarsen stone; like those at Stonehenge. Limestone is found around the Yorkshire dales, sandstone in Dorset, and the Isle of Iona, Tiree and Skye hold seams of luminous Scottish marble. Knowing the geological structure of the land you live on or visit, will give you greater understanding of the energetic frequency of a place, but also the guardian spirits that reside within the land, as they will all be unique to the natural materials they live within.

At the beginning of my journey with ancient fayerie, as I explored the subtle spiritual energies at sacred sites, I often sat in Chalice Well Gardens at the base of the Tor in Glastonbury. The Tor has been a scared pilgrimage site for centuries. The holy grail, used at the last supper of Jesus Christ, is rumored to be buried somewhere around the red and white spring near Chalice Well. As I rested at the Chalice Well, I would contemplate the immense peace that resides there. The energy surrounding this area has built up over the years. Not only is Chalice Well seated directly beneath the Tor, with powerful telluric energy lines running through it, but the energy grows from the pilgrims who visit to pray, send healing, and find peace. If something is honored to an extent, it will increase in energy from those who send it their love, faith, and peaceful thoughts.

Looking beyond surface level, the energy at sacred sites is potent and grows, since they are revered as sacred. Anything that has enough love poured onto it will eventually exude a loving vibration, and anything that is worshiped with peaceful energy will emanate more peace. So, the energy at sacred places grows every day with each passing pilgrim. Every time land is looked upon in wonder, or has silent prayers or ceremony held upon it, the land increases in divine energy. This energy becomes so strong that it will never dissipate, but last for eternity. Sacred places are not just special because of the telluric energy lines, and underground streams they are built on, or the star constellations they align with, or the mysteries they hold, or because of the unusual fayeries that gather around them; but because they grow daily in energy through awe, love, prayer, and wonder, thanks to the people who visit, making them powerhouses of divine contemplation and mystery.

Code of ethics when visiting sacred sites

Candles and Fires – Lighting fires at sacred sites can be dangerous and harm the land, the grass, and possibly the wildlife. Candle wax can leave a mess and is not biodegradable, and others may wish not to see this.

Ceremony and Prayer – You may feel inclined to perform a ceremony on the land. This may involve prayer for healing and unity. Individuals may work alone or in groups, sending prayers of compassion and peace to people or animals who are suffering, the Elven, and ancient fayerie of the land.

Custodian – Take care of the hallowed springs, the holy wells, the sacred sites. Tidy them up, clear them of rubbish, protect and care for them all, carrying the light of God in your heart.

Discernment – Be discerning when walking on powerful sacred land or ancient burial grounds.

Grounding – Sacred sites are powerhouses that can affect our energy in a profound way; be aware of feeling ungrounded or a little spaced-out at these places. Remember to ground yourselves. These powerful sites can help heal, nourish, and rebirth an individual's soul.

Offerings – Leave offerings of a biodegradable nature, such as a pinch of herb, berries or nuts, bird seed, a piece of your hair, a song, or a prayer. People love to leave offerings as a way of saying thank you to the ancestors, and the ancient fayerie. Make sure it is an honorable offering – something that will respect the place and people who visit the site after you.

Permission – When entering a sacred site, ask permission from the guardians who resides there. If the answer is yes, walk ahead. But in some cases, such as a tomb, the spirits of the place may not wish people to enter, or a person may not be ready to experience the intense energy that the place holds, so you may feel a "no" in your mind, indicating not to enter. Certain sites are abodes of the dead, and the feelings at these places can be powerful. The ancient fayerie protect your energy by letting you know not to enter the sites because they may be too dense or powerful for a person's sensitivity at that time in their lives – especially if you are feeling ungrounded or unwell.

Leave no trace – Take all litter home with you. Leave no trace that you visited.

Remembering the Ancestors – Take time to reflect on how the ancient ancestors walked the earth, the animists, and healers from the distant past, and how they connected to the spirit of place. And the first nation peoples who live on the land today, who honor the earth in everything they do, and who remember our place amongst the stars.

Tintagel Castle, Tintagel, Cornwall, England

Merlin's Cave, Tintagel Haven, Tintagel, Cornwall, England

Bears Head Rock, Tintagel Haven, Tintagel, Cornwall, England

St Nectan's Glen Waterfall, Trethevy, Tintagel, Cornwall, England

The Dragon of Boscastle, Cornwall, England

The Friendly Giant of Boscastle, Cornwall, England

The Tor, Glastonbury, Somerset, England

Chalice Well Gardens, Glastonbury, Somerset, England

Stonehenge, Salisbury, Wiltshire, England

The Stone of Destiny, The Hill of Tara, County Meath, Ireland

The Giant's Causeway, County Antrim, Northern Ireland

The Giant's Causeway, County Antrim, Northern Ireland

The Ring of Brodgar, Stenness, Orkney

Standing Stones of Stenness, Stenness, Orkney

Standing Stones, Avebury, Wiltshire, England

Munro Mountains, The Highlands, Scotland

St Columba's Bay, Isle of Iona, Scotland

St Columba's Bay, Isle of Iona, Scotland

Section II

Encounters with Ancient Fayerie in the Celtic Landscapes

"Let us go forth, the tellers of tales, and seize, whatever prey the heart long for, and have no fear. Everything exists, everything is true, and the earth is only a little dust under our feet."
William Butler Yeats

When I venture on pilgrimage, stillness penetrates my soul as I reach wild untamed places. I seek tranquillity on these passages through time. My mind empties with each step I take, and serenity eclipses me. The fair folk connect through a peaceful and loving heart; this may be why they visit frequently when I take pilgrimage walks. I sense joy when I receive glimpses into worlds from across the veil – worlds that are beyond my comprehension, but these sightings of fayerie are fleeting, lasting only seconds, so then in meditative dream like states, my imagination takes over, and stories pour forth from my heart. Stories of the Otherworlds of Elven, trolls, and mermaids, which I experience in a place in-between my vision and imagination, in a place beyond magic. A belief in the ancient fayerie teaches me to have reverence for the earth.

I have collated ten short fantasy stories from my travels across England, Scotland, and Ireland where I met with the People of Peace. I visited nemetons that have been used as places of ceremony and worship since time immemorial, where a sense of antiquity emanates from the entire area of land, allowing me to experience sacred subtle energies which radiate as feelings of bliss. It was in these places that my creative imagination took me on journeys to meet with Elven tribes who gathered in communities, dragon spirits guarding sacred rocks, trolls basking in woodlands, and fayeries dancing on moonbeams within time-honoured stone circles, each sharing their stories of peace and how they protect Mother Earth by living in simplicity, travelling gracefully within the flow of life. Lessons from which the human folk could surely gain wisdom. Once you have read these creative fantasy stories – then take to your own pilgrimage walks and create your own time-honoured tales of mystery and wonder.

The People of Peace

In the human realm, time and tide wait for no man. But in the land of enchantment, time lasts for eternity, and the tide... well, it is almost motionless, apart from the gentle brush of swell over beached land. It was one such day, when the rain cascaded down upon the Isle of Iona and the wind blew in gales – not the most perfect day for walking. But then again, I always considered the weather patterns to be part of my pilgrimage walk in the Highlands, especially on this holy isle, sometimes known as Druid Isle, or Iona, originally meaning Yew Place.

I stomped over the grassy machair towards St Columba's Bay, or Bay of New Beginnings, where rock changes form into gnomes and trolls. Colum Cille landed on this Bay in the year 563, and made Iona his home from thereon in. He built an Abbey on its sacred ground, and it became the birthplace for early Christianity in Scotland, England, and mainland Europe. The sacred manuscript, the Book of Kells, was also birthed on this holy Isle, after Colum Cille had passed to the heavenly realms.

That morning, I felt called to take the pilgrimage whatever the weather. My heart seemed to have an invisible thread pulling me to the place where time-honoured rocks stood waiting to tell tales of our ancestors. On my walk, I met not one single person. And anyone who has taken this walk knows that by the time one reaches the loch – Loch Stanoig – it can seem overwhelmingly eerie being all alone on the boggy pathway, with random shadow people flitting by. This area has been a place of ancient settlement, I'm sure of it. With only sheep as company – I could sense the spirit of Vikings and Monks in the heathered land. There was a remoteness that made me feel like I was walking towards the end of the world.

I eventually made it across the boggy, rain-soaked path until I came to a view that takes my breath away every time, I see it.

There in front of me was St Columba's Bay, with its weather-beaten billion-year-old cliff rocks standing at each end of the beach, almost hugging the landscape in a warm accepting embrace. I did feel welcome here, there was no doubt about it. The seclusion of the place was always welcoming. Being alone does not always mean being lonely. I was not surrounded by human folk, but it appeared I was not alone.

After another trek, passing about ten or so gently grazing sheep, I came to the stony beach at St Columba's Bay. Anyone who has trekked to this place will know the feeling of exuberance and relief at reaching this captivating destination which feels like being at the edge of the world, as if one could fall over the landscape's edge. Anyway, I had made it. My feet were a little soggy, my hair windswept and wild, but I felt free. My heart was happy. I felt I had reached home in a sense – my Otherworldly home.

How I stayed at this rocky forefront for so long, I have no idea. Some four hours passed by so quickly, when I had only intended to stay for about half an hour at most. But this is what happens when one walks on a thin place, which Iona is known as. A place where time stands still. My eyes fell dreamily on the stones on the shoreline – there were red ones, pink ones, green ones, and white ones. I bent down to pick one of the radiant green marble stones and held it close to my heart for a short time.

In that twinkling of time, remembering that I was all alone in this remote spot on the island and hadn't seen one person in several hours, I unexpectedly felt someone walk past me, like a gentle breeze blowing from behind. I felt nervous because I could not see anyone there; not anywhere. But you know when someone has walked past you, don't you?

I almost turned and said "hello," but instead I carried on holding the bright green stone, as a kind of talisman to keep me safe. I breathed a deep sigh, trying to relax, when I sensed a shadow pass me again. This was not a dark shadow, like those in horror movies; it was a spark of light. Swiftly, as the wind danced around the beached rocks, I overheard singing – a gentle, melodious tune from the most alluring voice I had ever heard. If I had been on a sofa back at home, I'm sure I would have fallen asleep, as the sound was similar to a lullaby, luring one's mind to enter into fayerie realm.

This song carried on and I didn't fall asleep, my mind transported me to a place of the deepest peace, as though a thousand doves had flown by and blessed my spirit; a peace that is experienced by hermit monks after spending months in solitude communing with God. Or how I imagine they would experience peace, as I have not personally tried hermitting for months in solitude... yet.

I turned around again, only this time I saw an angelic mermaid creature. She had long, flowing, silver blonde hair, and her whole body was pearlescent; she glowed brightly in gentle pastel colours, and was an elemental who carried an everlasting spectrum of light. My soul was transfixed. I didn't question if she was real, as I was too caught up in the moment, and had entered another reality that I trusted with all my heart. Her song echoed with ancient remembering. I recollect it vividly to this day.

I was shown that mermaids live on all continents, and take care of the coastline beaches, and you too may see one as you saunter on golden sand. This angelic being had a tale to tell. She stretched her hand out towards me and I reached out my hand towards her. Our fingertips touched, and as they did, I saw another flash in my mind. I was transported to an area of seawater past the Isle of Islay, far, far out to an area of ocean near the coast of Ireland. My imagination took me on a journey to the North Atlantic waters that surrounds Ireland; where a race of beings lived that knew about true fellowship. It was a city of Sidhe, of Elven ones, also known as the People of Peace, who all fayerie races are related to. There were merfolk who showed me they had come from the south of the world, from lost ancient landscapes, and had settled on nearby Irish, and Scottish shorelines because these lands are such special sanctuaries. These fayerie races come from all over the world and travel through the Celtic fayerie portals.

There were castles of gold and temples of starlight in this city, and the elementals were a brilliant array of colours, all singing songs of peace. They told me that they often gathered in circles and prayed for peace. Their race, which were of the merfolk Elven tribes, were sent to Earth to watch over, and care for the sea life. The seals are the loyal creatures of the oceans and they follow the mermaids wherever they travel, as their greatest friends. Rather like we have dogs, mermaids have sea dogs, seals, and they all live harmoniously in community, sharing life together.

There were no power figures who ruled these cities, every race of Elven souls have different degrees of intelligence and are acknowledged as having individual wisdom to share. The Elven types are guides who dwell in the depths of thought, sharing light language and there are Elven souls who are from the ancient stars, called the shining ones, who's light illuminates with ancient knowing, they are the wisest of all the Elven ones. The merfolk share insights in their own ways, too.

The mermaid tells me there are many People of Peace that live in the world, scattered in the hills, forests, woodland, and mountain ranges. The People of Peace is another term used for the Sidhe beings, the Elven ones who dwell in the depths of the emerald hills and mounds of Eire. They are the keepers of peaceful earth, where they pray and chant for harmony to reign over the landscapes, and much can be learnt in their presence if one is shown. But these stories are to be shared on another day, sat around a fire with tea and marshmallows, toasting by the flames.

Still holding the luminous green marble rock close to my

heart, I kissed it, and placed it back on the pebbly shoreline. I returned many times to St Columba's Bay, but never saw the mermaid again. Perhaps her spirit had travelled deep into the ocean, and there she now rests.

Until now, I have not spoken about this story to many, but it was time to tell the tale about the People of Peace, who live in many parts of the world. The ancient Sidhe who have travelled far and wide and exist in exquisite places around the globe, not just on these Celtic lands. It is a worldwide tribe, and you and I are connected to them by being a part of this sacred earth. People are now sharing their stories of encounters with the unseen world. It bonds the world of magic with that of the ordinary; it beholds a feeling that one can sum up in the word "unity," as there is no gap between nature and us humans. There never was. The People of Peace and Elven tribes wish to live again in harmony with you and me, and nature. I wonder how we can all walk forward together, as a People of Peace. I will leave that up to you to contemplate a while.

The Basalt Troll of Giant's Causeway

If you have ever been to Giant's Causeway in County Antrim on the north coast of Ireland, you will feel a sense of mystery about the place. The spirit of the place sings a precious tune, for there are giants who live in the rocks. They are troll-like giants. Trolls of basalt form. These stone beings are related to the basalt trolls of Fingal's Cave on Staffa Island, near Iona, which is the same geological structure of basalt lava columns which houses Giant's Causeway, both formed some 60 million years ago.

It has been spoken about through whispers in time that the ancient druid priests would visit Fingal's Cave – also known as "Uamh Binn" or "cave of melody" – sailing through the aquamarine Iona Sound from their home on Iona to perform initiations at the Isle of Staffa, where primeval trolls live.

These giants have guarded the sacred portals of Iona and the gateways to Ireland for millions of years. Some have been trapped in time by magic spells, unable to move until the sorcery was broken and they could again, range freely across the azure sea between Scotland and Ireland, between the areas where the basalt columns were formed.

The Celtic fayerie kingdoms are interconnected, and their subtle energies have created the vast landscapes. The Elven ones are earths guardians who protect the land, and often share profound wisdoms.

There was once a sorrowful troll who lived on Giant's Causeway, for his lifeforce had been taken away by wizardry and he had become suspended in time, unable to shapeshift from the spot he had been sitting at for thousands of years. His name was Moonless, for he was as black as the night sky when the moon was in hiding. He had a love affair with a basalt troll named Ebony, who lived on the Isle of Staffa. Her heart belonged to him and his to her, but an ancient spell had left them permanently frozen, unable to visit one another across the ocean's path. Their hearts pined, and Moonless became melancholy. Bitterness gripped his heart. Negativity brewed within his soul towards the witch who had placed the spell.

One fine day, the sun glistened upon the tranquil ocean. Ripples in the tide gently ebbed and flowed around the rocks of Giant's Causeway. Yet, the basalt troll sat in chains; a heavy cloud encompassed him; silence eclipsed his mind. Within the gentle swell of the Atlantic that day, swam a young seal. This graceful creature twisted, turned, danced, and meandered in the waters. After a few hours of swimming, she decided it was time for a snooze, so she hopped onto the geometric rock nearby the troll. She rolled onto her back, flippers gaping either side of her voluptuous tummy, the sun's rays warmed her.

As she basked in joy, she inquisitively turned her head and noticed Moonless. Her heart could not understand his sadness, and she saw his pain as she gazed into his sombre eyes. "Why are you sad?" she hummed softly.

The troll went on to tell the tale of his heartbreak from the witch's spell, distress filled his eyes as he shared the burden he had been carrying for thousands of years. The seal looked on aghast, tears formed in her heart as she felt the forlorn creature's sorrow. "Was the witch sad, too?" She tried to console him with her spoken thoughts. "Does her heart needs forgiving?"

The troll seemed rightfully furious. "What heart?" he rasped. How could he ever forgive such a spiteful priestess?

The seal murmured sweet innocent words which were filled with comfort, but they only enraged the troll even more so. "Maybe love eclipsed her, maybe her heart grew cold. Let go of this dreadful past," she sang her thoughts aloud, whilst flapping her flippers in delight. This soul knew only joy, and was wise for a young seal.

A frown appeared upon the troll's brow. "Let go, how?" he grimaced.

The seal, whose name was Grace, grew thoughtful for a second. "You could start by forgiving the witch. Gently let go of the past, just as the tide falls. Remember who you are. You are a kind basalt troll; love yourself, just as the oceans love the rain."

The troll thought for an exceptionally long time – it seemed to last for eternity, as hours of thought passed. The young seal had hit a nerve. All the while, Grace lay as flat as a pancake, gazing lovingly, never taking her eyes of the broken beast. She held space in his loneliness and waited for him to recover.

As the days rolled by, the troll's heart did soften. After thousands of years, he let in a deep love that the pure-hearted, persistent seal had shown to him. Moonless's eyes began to sparkle and a tear fell free into the ocean. His heart was softening to possibilities, and as it did, he began to forgive the witch. In doing so, he began to love himself. As this happened, a miraculous thing occurred. The chains that had surrounded him broke free and he was finally able to move. Grace, who was still residing in the presence of Giant's Causeway, flapped her flippers. "See?" she said. "You had the power all along to break the magic spell. The power to love is all that was needed."

Days passed, and the heavy cloud lifted from Moonless. He forgave, and in doing so, began to love himself again. No magic in the whole world has any power over the heart. Not ever. And so, the story of the giant troll at the causeway was re-written.

Grace visited her friend regularly, and last I heard, the troll changed his name to Moon, for now he felt illuminated in light and was never moonless again. He reunited with his soul mate, Ebony, at Fingal's Cave, who had also been set free from the ancient sorcery. Harmony reigned at Giant's Causeway, and I think it is like that to this day.

A petite fayerie told me this tale, she appeared as a spark of light whilst I walked the heathered hills of Iona. This fayerie sprang from the lilac heather, and revealed revelations of heavenly changes in the land. People visit Giant's Causeway and pray for peace on earth. Prayers of peace penetrate the land, and last for eternity. Nothing dark can exist in the presence of love; it is the most potent frequency in the universe.

The Golden City of Skye

Deep in the heart of the Cuillin mountains on the Isle of Skye, in Scotland, lives a rare pink marble which belongs to the fairies. The fairies not only created the land, but gave it its colour, too. They decided to make pretty formations in the rocks with pistachio greens, delicate pinks, and cream colours with wisps of black, forming what we know as Skye marble. This marble is part of the geology of the Cuillin mountains of Skye. But that is not the only thing to be found on this Isle – also known as "the Isle of Mists" – for there are iridescent pools which glisten opalescent hues of ultramarine, where the fair folk gather and rest, there are ancient and mysterious fayerie glens, and the mountain ranges look as if they are straight out of a fantasy film.

Trekking through the vast natural landscape of the Cuillin mountains which span across many kilometres. One is met with a raw and abundant feeling of freedom, the wide-open spaces, and awe-inspiring Munro mountains are a sight to behold. Certain landscapes of the Cuillin region are akin to walking into a scene from the *Lord of the Rings*, a place where you would envisage Gandalf with his crystal staff in hand, pilgrimaging across the valleys to visit tribes of Elven elders, who together would share akashic wisdoms, whilst rooted next to standing stones made of amethyst quartz, while white elk stand guarding secrets of the land, their horns saturated in gold. But I digress. On this walk, the violet-coloured heather gathered around the rocks, and one could hear the hushed chatter of fayerie folk, where other dimensions await the discerning traveller and where celestial light is brought to life in fayerie form. There are individual elemental gateways along these mountain passes, some of these veer off towards the Scottish seelie courts, and each gateway guards a quintessence of treasure, which the seeker meets as they cross this wild terrain.

As I trekked further along the rugged landscape, I melded with the pure earthly vibrations emanating from this sacred Isle, and my soul came home to itself. It was late summer, and I was ambushed by hundreds of midges who feasted upon my bare skin. But they were a mild irritation in comparison, as my mind was eclipsed by the *genius loci* of the land. I sat on a boulder rock, took out my water bottle, and refreshed myself. Beauty filled my eyes as I relished the view. When out of nowhere appeared the most charming Elven spirit. He was adorned in a pale cerulean suit, his hair was flowing white, upon which he wore a headband of ornate Celtic silver weave. His eyes twinkled and beheld the knowledge of a few thousand years, and I foresaw his name as Aelfdene, which means "from the elfin valley." His hand reached out to help me stand from the boulder rock, and abruptly I dissipated from human form and transformed into a maiden in a long, flowing white dress with a silver rope belt around my waist. I was journeying without effort.

The spirit of this place is beyond magical. Most who visit Skye will have fayerie ancestors in their ancient history and recognise this Isle as home. This wild land will restore your weary spirit, and where you may feel defeated from life, it will empower your soul with a remembering of where you stood and, with courage, embodied light throughout all lifetimes. You kept returning to fulfil a prophecy, until luminous peace was restored on earth; a time when all nations remembered in their hearts a truth of life in all universes.

This life's journey has been challenging for many, but the Elven ones – who's souls are descended from you and I, and who live in the magical places over the earth – remind us of our heritage and souls' strength. The quintessence of light is grander than the negative energies that exist on the earth plain, but for a long time one was unable to survive without the other. Particles within the energetic light spectrum now spontaneously combust and allow an increased radiance to exist on earth, in an elevated frequency. Humanity evolves through the cosmic changes. These earth changes were seen in prophetic visions from times in early civilisations where the fayerie clans co-existed together in harmony. These times are now re-emerging in a contrasting frequency, and each one of you carries the wisdom of illumination within your soul.

So, the gentle Elven soul led me through a golden passageway, and I entered another realm that left me speechless. My heart spoke from thereon in, and his heart spoke to me. The elemental worlds communicate foremost through the heart's voice, for it is the voice of truth that no-one can doubt or deny. Aelfdene walked me to a golden carriage, and I stepped into it. As I did so, the carriage and its silver sheen ponies galloped off into the distance. We rode through a rose-coloured mist that somehow felt familiar. I trusted Aelfdene, but I was bewitched.

We carried on through the fine pink mist until we came to a clearing. Within this clearing beheld a golden city with hundreds of fair folks going about their day; it was authentic fayerie land, and I have never seen such wonder. There were castles built in crystal and metallic silver, a spectrum of rainbow flowers grew freely on the roadsides. The city shimmered brightly and dazzled in beauty. We travelled further along a quartz crystal roadway until we finally reached another destination.

The Elven soul stepped out of the carriage, with graceful moves he reached for my hand, and I ascended onto the pathway, as the satin gown I wore, caressed the curves on my body. There before us gathered the gentle folk, the shining ones, and the People of Peace, the dragons, the gnomes, and the merfolk. The fayerie tribes assembled in their sparkling regalia. The Elven come together in sacred places to enchant, feast, share wisdom, and celebrate. Aelfdene confessed through his heart that this land was a place of homecoming to our true Elven natures. It was my homecoming and your homecoming, where our souls reignite. All were welcome at this place, where the energy glistens so brilliantly.

I stayed what seemed like forever in this place, observing the celebration from afar, aware I didn't want to be caught in fayerie time forever. But the lure is always strong, you see. Food was gifted to me, but I politely refused it, as fayerie food does not always agree with humans. I received hugs of angelic embrace, though; I felt reverence in this place.

The diverse elementals danced way into midnight, and I cherished the scene in front of me. Their world is different to ours and there are things I do not fully understand, but they ignited a light in my human soul. Finally, I was ushered back into the ornate carriage and Aelfdene escorted me back through the golden city, where the celestial beings now slept. We travelled through the deep rosy mist until we reached the point where I began my journey. Aelfdene told me to carry the strength of starlight within me – when the darkness of the world felt overwhelming – to remember this place. Our communication continued through the heart, as I was rendered speechless.

The timeline faded and I found myself standing by the lichen-covered rock. Gradually I hiked back through the heathered pathways, mesmerised by this encounter. To have connected with the Elven soul was a blessing indeed. Communicating through the heart will transport you to cities of gold that exist in the Otherworlds. The heart will allow you to penetrate the earth's knowledge. Everything is revealed if we trust our intuitive wisdom and remember who we are – not just human souls, but perhaps part-fayerie. Are encounters with the fayerie realm pure escapism, wild imagination, or of visions beyond the veil? I like to think of these moments as a mixture of all three. I believe in all possibilities. For whom are we mere mortals to disbelieve in magic?

The Dragon of Boscastle and the Friendly Giant

Boscastle, known in the Cornish language as Kastel Boterel, is a small fishing village in Cornwall. It is a place that is steeped in magic from throughout the ages. Cornwall is known for its giants and little people, and many tales are told of such. Boscastle is an enchanting place of witches, wizards and black cats, and there are tales of wee fayeries who inhabit the nearby woods, who ride on the backs of wild deer at night and are sometimes spotted by local dog walkers. There are also fishermen and good-natured village folk who do not believe in magic at all.

It was on a cold stormy night that Bill, a kindly fisherman from Boscastle, went to check on his boat that had come loose from its moorings in the tiny harbour. He quickened his walking pace along the harbour's edge as the rain lashed down hard on his face. His boat was free floating and bashing around in the raging sea. Bill looked on in angst as his beloved fishing boat was being eaten by the ravishing waves. In all his days, he had never seen a storm as fierce as this.

He stood on the harbour's edge but was finding it impossible to get his balance in the storm, when a sudden gust of wind blew Bill into the ocean. As the current whipped around him, Bill was dragged at incredible speed to the sea floor. "Oh Lord," he anxiously thought, then looked up and prayed, all he could envisage were murky waters. He realised this could be his last night alive, and he thought of his cosy cottage and its warm fireside where Teddy the Labrador lay awaiting his return. Bill had a hearty stew cooking on the stove, waiting to be devoured by both Teddy and him. He could not possibly meet his maker this dark evening; he had plans for a quiet night, reading to Teddy by the fireside.

In those moments of despair Bill felt weightless and saw whisps of light glistening through the sea. Bill thought the angels along with God had come to greet him, when suddenly, an emerald dragon's face appeared under the turbulent water and gazed at him with piercing golden eyes that shone with love. He nudged Bill with his gigantic nose, and the fisherman froze solid.

To his left, he witnessed a giant, with a long pointy nose and spindly chin, whose eyes glistened kindness like the sun. *How can it be?* Bill thought. He wondered whether he should be more afraid of his ultimate drowning or of these magical beasts that swam next to him.

In that second the giant reached out his extra-large fingers and grabbed Bill by his pullover, lifting him out of the stormy ocean, and placed him gently on the harbour's edge. Bill lay motionless, quite unable to move his exhausted, wet body; he was in complete shock. He stared back into the treacherous sea, but the emerald dragon and giant were nowhere to be seen. Bill was safe and out of danger, but all the while he wondered if what he had experienced had been real. Nevertheless, he was grateful to be alive. Shaken by the accident, he tilted his head up at the night-sky, clasped his hands together in prayer to thank God for his life.

Bill returned home a little shell-shocked, but grateful. Later that evening, he got to fulfil his wish of a quiet night in. After composing his thoughts, he dried himself off, gathered two bowls of his hearty stew, and placed one on the floor for Teddy. Bill sat by the fireside, drew his companion close and read a story as a sense of peace washed over him. Teddy relaxed, too, as his master had returned home safe and sound.

In the days that followed, Bill told many people about the night the ocean almost took his life, and how a friendly giant and dragon had saved him. And even when people laughed at his tale, Bill smiled to himself. He came to realise it was only those with magic in their soul who believed his story. Occasionally, they also saw these majestic guardians, guarding the sea at Boscastle.

To this day, the dragon and the friendly giant silently protect the fishermen at this quaint little harbour. If you look closely enough, you too will see them both at rest in the rocks.

The Gnome in the Stone

The twilight hour is when the ancient fayerie visit. This hour is when they pass between worlds, when they make mischief in our homes and enchant under the stellar rays, creating fayerie rings under sleeping oak trees. It was in this hour that I was in deep slumber, dreaming peacefully; quite a novelty for me to sleep so soundly. But around 4.30am, I heard a sound. My eyes flashed open, and I became wide awake.

I have a rock – a sky-coloured calcite stone – which resides on my dressing table, calcite being a stone of serenity. I gazed at the jewel, when to my astonishment, I saw a petite figure standing over it. It was not a usual fayerie-looking creature with wings, but he had a round face with plump cheeks. He was adorned in a fine aquamarine suit, smart trousers, and a jacket with a checked shirt underneath. This being beamed at me, and I have never seen such a welcoming grin.

Wondering if I was still asleep and dreaming, I became intrigued by my vision. I requested, rather bluntly, "Who are you?" "Peter," he replied quite boldly. "Peter is my name." He jumped out from the cerulean rock and stood on the carpet, staring at me. Incidentally, the carpet was blue as well, so he kind of blended into the background with ease.

Scared to blink in case he disappeared, I watched with amazement. I realised I had stopped breathing, so I proceeded to take a few intense breaths before I fainted. Peter then proceeded to strut around my abode, inspecting every nook and cranny of my home, his bottom waddled as he did.

A feeling of serenity washed over me. Peter glanced over at me, his eyes twinkled brighter than precious diamonds and, as if hypnotised for a second, I drifted into an altered state of mind. Peter was showing me his habitat, his world. I envisioned a place where there were many rocks and many gnomes bumbling about their day. Gnomes care deeply about everything, rather like kindly fusspot grandmothers checking everyone is stocked up on tea and biscuits, filling children's bellies with candy.

They are rock solid companions – excuse the pun. They are loyal, and once they find their person, they will probably stay with them for life, even moving lodgings if that person moves home. Gnomes are silent guides, as they lovingly watch over you while you sleep, taking care to guard your sanctuary space from other Pixi types who only want to steal your food or move your objects.

Every stone throughout the world carries the essence of gnome energy.

Peter carried on daydreaming, sharing his world until my eyes began to close mid-vision. I fell back into a deep sleep and awoke a few hours later.

I waltzed over to the dresser, placed my hand on the jumbo-sized calcite and for an instant I was transported back to the encounter with the gnome in the stone – or Peter, as he liked to be known in his glamour suit. I read later that Peter is derived from a Greek word, "Petros," meaning rock or stone, which seemed symbolic for the charming gnome. I had many sightings of Peter thereafter and I like to think he is the guardian of my home. Most of the time he rests inside the stone, where he awaits the twilight hour.

Next time you fall asleep, set your alarm for 4.30am. This time is known to some folk as psychosis hour, or fayerie hour, and you too may awaken to find that you have visitors of the Elven kind making mischief at your hearth.

The Midnight Elven Festival

It was a grey and misty nebulous morning when I visited an enchanting stone circle, near a bluebell woodland on the Isle of Albion. This nemeton is adorned with magic, and as I stood on the emerald grasses that surrounded these age-old stones, I could feel the ancient ones gather. I had dreamt of this place, once upon a time, long ago.

I have little expectation when visiting sacred sites, but I am often left astounded at the majestic energy these sites hold. But one must journey deep into the land, deep into the Otherworldly realms, beyond the veil of conscious thought. As I sauntered around the circle of stones, tenderly touching each one, I began to interpret their story. The sheep who rested amongst the stones, greeted me as I walked by. *They must be content on the spirited land*, I thought.

I carried on walking until one stone lit up in my presence as if saying, "listen to me." So, I did. The grand megalith drew me in. I lay against it, and as if in warm embrace, its energy gently held me.

My mind drifted into a serene state, when unexpectedly, I felt a spirit draw close. I opened my eyes – still leaning against the stone – and saw a ginormous troll being, some fifteen feet tall. This bonny troll had shapeshifted out of the ancient stone I rested against. He leant towards me, but I sensed no cause for alarm, for his aura was endearing and kindly. In a placid voice, he murmured, "welcome" as he leant out his chubby fingers towards me. I gently placed my tiny hand in his, and as I did, he proclaimed, "A celestial light brightens our encounter."

I felt safe, it was similar to being held by a kindly grandfather who would lead his granddaughter on an adventure. I trusted this Celtic giant, or troll, as they are known as. Most trolls are not elegant looking – some can look gnarled and ancient, some frightening looking, but they do not wish to alarm people with their appearance. In all my days, I have never come across a hard-hearted troll. They take you under their wing and are affectionate beings; they are the gentle giants of the Celtic landscapes.

So, with my hand in his, I went on a journey in my imagination to a stone circle in a timeline past and was shown the place I was standing at. It looked different, with many Elven, fayeries, dragons, and trolls, all gathered at this time-honoured site. Dusk fell and many fires were lit. The Elven and their fayerie relatives shared a bounty of food and drink. I smelt the strong scent of honey lingering in the air, a sweet and enticing aroma; I imagine it was mead being shared. I overheard cheering and laughter, and knowledge was being spoken of by the shining ones. These shining ones are the Elven souls from the furthest stars, and they carry immense insight and teachings.

The atmosphere buzzed with merriment. Rabbits, hedgehogs, field mice, moles, voles, bats, owls, hares, and other creatures all joined the festivities. Harps were playing; melodious tunes floated through the air. I witnessed a portal forming in the distance, an entry point to where the Elven tribes and their relatives travelled from all over the world to this magical site. Hawaiian Elven, Icelandic Elven, French fayeries, trolls from the Himalayas, sparkling white dragons from Siberia, moss green Elven from New Zealand, fair folk from every different culture were visiting the festival. It dawned on me this midnight festival was much more than a party to share blessed friendship and celebration. It was a gathering of Elven nations.

The Elven gathered from around the earth to share concepts on healing arts, magic, and shapeshifting techniques to help heal the planet – you name it, no Elven art was left unshared. This was a festival of light where I envisioned the Elven and fayerie sat in circle sharing insights about global peace, their prayers raised the vibrations of Mother Earth. As they sang songs of peace.

My eyes dazzled at the stone troll. His eyes softened and

beamed deeply into mine. Nodding his head in acknowledgement of what I had witnessed, we stood in silence for a few moments longer, watching the midnight festivities of the Elven races until the timeline faded.

The troll bent down and dug beneath the grass to where he was hiding treasure, and pulled out three acorns, placing them at my feet. They were a gift – a symbol of golden wisdom. I understood the acorns were symbolic of strength and potential, and to the ancient druids, they were oak knowledge. I gave the troll some almonds I had been keeping in my pocket, ready as sacred offerings for the fair folk. He held the wee nuts and smiled affectionately, bowing his head.

Placing his new treasure in a secret hole, he covered the almonds with mud and grass, before turning to look at me once more. His eyes sparkled brightly, and in a flash, he was gone. His essence had shapeshifted back into the standing stone which stood by my side.

I leant against the rock, closed my eyes and rested for a moment longer, dwelling in the blissful energies of the land. I knew one day I would return to this place and perhaps meet with the troll being once again.

Barney, the Shapeshifting Troll

There he stood, towering above the emerald terrain, a troll, some twenty-feet high. I had never noticed him before, although I sometimes walk that way to view the ocean and glance out over the cliffs landscape in Cornwall. The whereabouts of this giant will remain hidden, as many fayerie do not wish to be disturbed, and before sharing any fayerie story, one must ask their permission first, this troll being did not mind his story being shared, but his abode was to remain a secret. He appeared, to be seen and recognised as part of the environment with all its wild ruggedness. I invited him to share his name, and he continued to take me on a grand journey explaining why he had the nickname he had.

His voice rumbled gently, "I am Barney, short for Barnaby." He informed me he lived in a barnacle on the seashore's rocks and had magical powers to shapeshift into whatever size he wanted. To prove his words, he disappeared – and I envisioned him in a tiny barnacle – then he reappeared to converse some more.

I gifted him a daffodil, and he reached out his enormous hand to accept the cheerful floret. Gently holding the blossom, he twirled around in adoration of the golden gift. My heart beamed with affection, and his spirit softened. I was in awe of this gentle giant.

I have met few prickly trolls in my day; most are kind-hearted, a bit odd looking, and always ready to share tales of their world and what secret treasure's they are hoarding. I have come to realise the treasure a troll keeps is always a medley of nuts, berries, occasionally crystals, and stones.

Barney did have a tale. He told me of a place beyond the spiritual veil, of where a dragon once lived on this shoreline and had been caught in sorcery that left him forever stranded in the rocks. It was a dreadful curse placed on the dragon thousands of years ago by a Celtic tribe that lived on these lands. The tribe became dark after a spiritual war had taken place between angels, demons, and fayerie.

Barney pointed over to the headland and I stared, eyes wide. As sure as day, I saw a noble dragon laying peacefully in the landscape. Yet this poor dragon had chains around his body, unable to move, he had been ordered to guard a secret. The troll's storytelling began, as he shared the tale of what had happened all those years ago, and of how sacred lands had been overtaken by a strange spiritual shadow, but of how this shadow was lifting, as a light now shone on the earth so brightly that no darkness can exist in its presence. That spark was baptised love.

Illumination was returning, and all the earth was ascending through astral changes. There would be no more hiding from the truth, as the lands clear old, outdated programmes. He uttered these words whilst bouncing up and down on his feet, hands clasped together, feeling great excitement. The earth shook after each of his bounces.

Barney explained earth's story is being rewritten as a new light dawns on humanity. The dragons and the secrets they guard, are from far-off starlit places where the Sidhe originated from and co-existed with other Elven souls. Once the dragons rise, he stated, so too will the light codes that humanity once knew of, and these ancients secrets will again be shared freely. As the planet changes course, Earth will move into an era of luminescence where peace and tranquillity echoes throughout the ethers, and we are at the beginning of this unfamiliar journey.

A little flabbergasted, and shocked by what I heard, I stood in silence. Sparks began to fly nearby where the dragon lay and the chains around his weak body, began to break loose, discharging electrical light as it did. The earth's energy on the cliff rose slightly and then relaxed back down, and there in a puff of smoke stood the dragon in full glory. Stretching his wings and lashing his tail from side to side as he got ready to take flight, he was free.

As he ascended into the air invisible codes from the earth's matrix burst forth. A prism of pastel colours swirled in cloud formation, and unicorns, fayeries, and merfolk arose from the opaque light. It was alluring.

Peace echoed from the clifftop, and I began to understand the meaning of "a new light is dawning" – a suppression would lift from human folk as humanities shadow transforms, and the earths guardians, and mortals, would learn to co-exist side by side, just as they did thousands of years ago.

Not only were the nature spirits being released from a shadow that had eclipsed them, but so was humanity. The sight before me vanished into thin air and I was left with only memories. The landscape before me looked exquisite and, somehow, lighter in feeling.

Next time you go walking, be that near your home or even further afield, take note of the simple scenery. You may think that magic does not exist on your doorstep but believe me, it does. Within gardens, local parks, plain old grassy hill tops, they all hold unique codes of transformation. Stay for a while on these lands, close your eyes, and open your heart; enchanting stories await you.

A remembering of the old ways of ancient fayerie is buried deep in your heart, under layers of outdated, staunch ways of thinking. Within the Celtic wild, hidden beneath the geological structures of the headlands, the cliffs, and within the caves, is cryptic alchemy to feel into, trolls to acquaint with, fayeries to delight in, and dragon companions to embrace. Blink, and you will miss them.

The Cornish Woodland Troll

Countless nature spirits live in the wild. But only the ones you are destined to meet will appear. Once I met the spirit of a woodland troll. His soul gently appeared to me as I leant against a beech tree in a quaint woodland area in the heart of Cornwall. It was a mild weathered day at the beginning of springtime. A merriment of bluebells filled the wood, joyful echoes burst through their violet trumpets. And there I sat, amongst these violet beauties, to rest for a moment and eat a cheese sandwich.

He was five feet in height, dressed in a brown outfit that had twigs overflowing from its buttonholes, he wore stripy trousers, and was quite plump. His eyes were the colour of hazelnuts, his cheeks were rounded, and his tiny teeth appeared as he smiled a far-reaching grin. He bent down to touch my shoulder, just as a kindly grandpa would. There were no words exchanged, but his actions spoke louder than words.

The troll revealed in my visions, that during his time in the woodland, he sits quietly in the silver silence of the shadows, comfortable in the dark, wet, undergrowth, undisturbed by the light. He shares his gentleness with the animal kingdom and gifts the deepest healing to all beings.

Trolls transform all that is dark into light. Breaking down the barriers that need letting go of, and they are healing balm to your soul. Trolls are humble but be prepared to laugh as they are amusing. He hums Awen – the echo of inspiration, the melody of the forest, of the wind in the trees. He is as timeworn as the mountains and as enlightened as the stones. He is thoughtful and giving as the sun. A deep reverence emanates from trolls. They are loners, and one must give them the space they desire for them to shine in your presence.

He took deep breaths, as if showing me I too needed to breathe deeper. I did and my spirit calmed. I relaxed into the fathomless roots of the tree that were bulging out of the topsoil, where I sat. I was melding into the earth. I became her, and she became me. The troll stood by me all the while.

My mind became quiet, and I felt the heartbeat of the earth. In front of me a thin mist appeared, as I moved between spiritual dimensions. Sparks of light appeared from out of nowhere, and a badger wandered from behind a cluster of wildflowers. His nose twitched as he smelt the air and riding gallantly on his back was a petite fayerie clothed in black and white. *It must be his totem fayerie,* I thought.

Mice scuttled across the leafy floor of the woodland, and each sapling, blossom, and wild animal had a nature spirit devoted to them. There were tiny pixies, who are the Elven fayeries of Cornwall. Some of the nature spirits had elaborate wings; others were unusual in body shape; many appeared ancient. The troll was showing me his domain. Fayerie world unfiltered looks like a scene from the *Dark Crystal* movie, full of enchantment.

He was showing me a place beyond time, even though I cannot always perceive it. The earth is alive, and has guardians ensuring its protection, nurturing it diligently every day.

I sighed; and peace filled my heart, then I became thoughtful. How could an individual as slight as me help the earth with all of her complexities? The troll felt my concern and again placed his hand on my shoulder. Communicating through his heart, he advised "each change begins with the individual, through opening their heart, and transforming themselves. The land, the trees and the wild animals need attention. And every conscious decision you make encourages positive change; because it's the humble things you do, as no good deed is too trivial to make a difference."

My eyes watered, and a tear fell freeform down my cheek, and gently, he wiped away the tear. He stood by my side for a long while after, and we soaked up the tranquillity of the woodland.

After another spectacle of fayeries had passed by, he declared in a soft voice, "Remember me," and then he disappeared back into the essence of nature.

If you have been in the presence of a troll, you will know and remember. Time stands still. Trolls are peace eternal; they are the soul of the planet – the melody of Om. But they have often been misunderstood. Maybe one day you will meet one deep in the forest glen. If you do, hold out your hand and wait, and prepare for magic. It will happen.

The Enchanted Fayerie Glen

There are many enchanted places on the Isle of Albion, that will take your breath away and transport your imagination to the land of fayerie. When you walk on magical ground, your soul will ignite and you will feel bewitched for a moment, and lonely feelings will disappear, as you connect to the spirit of place. And you will feel as if you are in a time warp, as hours pass by, but they are literally just moments. This is when you know you are entering a wilderness that has been touched by the Elven ones.

Certain sanctuaries beguile you the moment you set foot on their hallowed soil. There was one such wooded glen that opened my heart more than any other. I trod softly on the moss-filled ground. The fayerie glen lay before me. I sensed the primordial Sidhe had blessed this land. Yet, the Sidhe are rarely seen, unlike their fayerie relatives, the dryads, and mushroom fayeries, who love to surprise the unsuspecting traveller. Rain-soaked grass covered this landscape, and a welcoming rowan tree stood by a dry-stone wall, abundant with character and scarlet berries. Rowan trees are most favoured by the fair folk, along with the ever-mysterious blackthorn, and hawthorn trees.

I advanced further into this mystifying wooded glen and discovered a ring of hawthorn trees that stood awaiting the inquisitive visitor. And, as I stepped into the circle of trees, my vision blurred, as I slipped into a meditative state of mind. I was transported through mists of time, and as swirls of fog settled around my body, a clearing was shown to me. In that space stood a colossal troll; he was a stone troll, towering in height.

These giants live in the landscapes amidst the trees that adorn this Otherworldly landscape. There are all kinds of trolls that live in the Celtic wild: forest trolls, bog trolls, mountain trolls. This one stood as a guardian to the entrance of this realm, inspecting my heart to see if I came in peace. If I did not, I would surely have been removed from the mist and transported back to human time. He allowed me to stay in fayerie time, for a while, and he whispered, "Welcome."

Now, although I was standing in a grove of hawthorn trees, the area had magically grown; it became a vast landscape that swept across acres in front of me. There was an air of trust between the troll and myself, and he ushered me to follow him down a light filled passageway. Along this avenue were a wealth of gateways, leading to individual Elven realms. I gazed far into the distance and realised it led to an area where dragons dwelt.

There were wee mushroom gnomes in cherry and white coloured jackets, skipping around my feet, three of them to be exact, they giggled and pushed my legs forward as if to keep me walking. They held their hands up to their mouths, whispering to each other, and chuckling, amused by my presence. It's a good job the fayerie believe in humans, or we wouldn't exist to them at all, imagine that!

The mushroom folk led me down a single path where violet florets adorned the area; the aroma was as sweet as sugar. Rabbits sat in pairs, bowing their heads as I walked on by. A butterfly landed on my hair and rested there for a while. Eventually, I came to an oak doorway, covered in emerald coloured ivy. The face of the Greenman appeared in its middle and this forest being grinned cheerfully at me.

The doorway opened. I entered a secret garden filled with a kaleidoscope of flowers. The scent overwhelmed me, and I sneezed. Each flower had its own fayerie embracing it. I stood, admiring the view, and the wee mushroom gnomes nudged my legs, beckoning me to rest on an exceptionally large fly agaric mushroom, for a while.

Dormice, silver grey rabbits, rosy robins, and ebony blackbirds gathered around. A ladybird landed on my hand and peered up at me. To my surprise, a heavy stone rolled over my foot and out leapt a gnome. The gnome wandered over to a golden fayerie, that seemed to be a part of a buttercup flower, and together they spoke in a language of light. He plucked a tiny snowdrop from the soil, held the flower up, and ran towards me. Then he tripped on a blade of grass, tumbled to his knees, rolled over three times in a somersault, and finally landed on his clumsy feet and passed the dainty blossom to me. "Everyone has a flower," he beamed.

Graciously, I accepted the symbolic relevance of the little flower bud and placed it gently on the ground for the fair folk to keep, I took some walnuts out of my pocket and placed them on the ground. The woodland creatures gathered to see the nuts, holding their hands to their hearts in delight. The individual walnuts were passed to the dormouse, the squirrel, and the mole, as all three waited patiently. Nothing goes to waste in the land of enchantment. I chanted a prayer to the good folk as a way of thanks. A melodious tune came from my heart, a light language I remember singing once in a far-off land.

It came time for me to return home, to my world. The mist dissipated, and the stone troll along with the humorous mushroom fayeries gently disappeared from my vision. I returned along the pathway and became aware of myself standing in the circle of hawthorn trees where my journey begun. How long I had been in the *Otherworld*, I have no idea.

Fayerie Glen's behold Albion's classical secrets. That day I left with a renewed faith in my heart, as in my mind a belief of the fayerie realm was undoubtedly so, for on my visit, I truly had been "away with the fayeries."

The Highland Dragons

It just so happens some days are more magical than others. Now, if every day were brimming with magic, we would not appreciate those days when true magic strikes. I will tell you the tale of one such day.

I passed on foot through a mountain range in the depths of the Highlands in Scotland. Awe-struck by the natural landscape. And as I wandered further into the heather filled pathways, peace overwhelmed my heart. I didn't feel alone, for in the stillness, a lingering presence overshadowed my mind. It felt both ghostly and fascinating, and I knew I was entering fayerie terrain.

I sauntered further along and came across a Munro Mountain that had me overcome with emotion. Water filled my eyes as a "God moment" eclipsed me. Those are times when the great mystery fills you with a magical essence.

Rooted to the spot for what seemed like eternity – my feet stood motionless, but it was only a few minutes in human time. The mountain towered above me, and there on top of the Munro was an enormous dragon, his scales were ruby red, and the golden sunlight shimmered of his back. He threw me an intense stare and I tried to hide my glances by pretending I hadn't seen him. But curiosity flooded my mind.

I peered at him again and he lifted his lip, his teeth appeared, and they glistened like pearls. My heart stopped for a moment. His eyes softened and his eyelashes fluttered, and I realised he was smiling at me.

His front paw beckoned me to move closer to him, which I did, but this took a while as I had to walk over a boggy heather-filled pathway to get closer to the bottom of the mountain (it is awfully hard to walk over boggy ground whilst looking upwards). Eventually, I came to a boulder stone and sat quietly for a rest, all the while my eyes transfixed on the ruby red dragon.

As I perched on the boulder, I was blown away with what happened next. The mountain before me became invisible and I could see straight through it. The image inside took my breath away. There was a ring of dragons, flying in a circling motion – a circle of protection over something I could not quite see. These dragons were all the colours of the rainbow, shimmering brightly. They did not notice me watching them, which I was relieved about.

Quite suddenly, as though there was an urgency about being noticed, a tiny dragon flew out of the centre of the mountain and landed at my feet. He was pale green and the most delightful thing I had ever seen. He was the size of a Labrador dog, but tiny for a dragon.

I asked him his name, but he did not answer, so I guessed. "Is it Emerald?" He took some deep breaths and tried to blow fire like the big dragons do – their way of communicating – but he only managed to splutter wet and snot all over me. Ugh.

Anyway, we kept on with the name-guessing game. "Is it Sparkle?" I continued to think of names that suited him, but I had to think hard to find a name he liked. "Is it Durin?" I asked. Well, his wings puffed out and he blew with all his might, just as a big dragon would! A cloud of smoke came out of his mouth and covered the nearby heather.

So, his name was Durin, which is Nordic and actually means mythical dwarf. He liked it. I laughed, still covered in his sticky wet breath.

I realised the mountain was a school for baby dragons. The senior dragons were teaching them about the ancient laws of dragonhood, a language of light, from the lore of the Sidhe, who took up residence in the Highlands thousands of years ago. They learnt about sacred dragon magic that no human would ever truly understand; we would, though, get glimpses. You see, people believe the giants and dragons of the land are dying and there are few left. But my tale will tell you otherwise. The giants, dragons, fayeries, and mermaids of the unseen world will always exist. They are eternal, just as your and my spirit; our souls live forever. The dragons will always be here.

After a while, it was time for me to leave this sacred place. I bade farewell to Durin and the ruby red dragon, but as I walked back up the boggy path, Durin plodded behind me, following my lead. I encouraged him to go back to the mountain, and I shrugged my shoulders at the ruby dragon, questioning what to do. Durin kept on following me.

I carried on my walk, thinking he would get bored and go home, but he did not. He was like a baby duckling who hadn't quite figured out who its mum was but would follow a leader. Eventually, the guardian dragon of the mountain got my attention and spoke these words, "This is now a guardian dragon of yours. Love and honour him; he will guard and heal the land where you live." *Wow*, I thought, *a dragon companion. How cosmic.*

The ruby red dragon's gentle murmurs echoed in my mind, he carried on his communication with me, "Beloved lady, these Celtic landscapes connect to the lost continents of Lemuria, and Atlantis – land's where starlit wisdom once echoed on Elven tongues, where companion dragons rode in celestite skies with fellow fayerie on their dragon saddles. These lands are a place to remember your Elven star lineage to the Dragon races and a heart centred bliss." His essence reverberated, and he peered with sincerity. "It is my wish for others to remember their connection to the dragon races and remember how their hearts sang a truth in ancient times." I listened intently, waiting for more words to pour forth from this majestic beast, but he went silent, I felt him retreat into the mountain, but before he disappeared, he spoke sweet words to me, "Dwell in happiness." Then he was gone.

The wilderness beholds the magic of the Tuatha De Danann, the Elven tribes, the dragon races, and our ancient ancestors. Fayerie land is a world which is perceived with the heart of a child.

Durin never left my side. My house is, of course, not quite big enough to house a dragon, so when I returned home, I went in search to find him accommodation. Eventually I found the perfect spot. He now lives on a cliff overlooking the ocean, and I go and visit him some days. So, you see, dragons live eternally in the unseen realms.

If you are out walking one day in the natural landscapes, you too may come across one, and it may follow you home. Just make sure you have a king-sized garden for it to sleep in and dogs to keep it company.

Conclusion

I am a wind in the sea,
I am a sea-wave upon the land,
I am the sound of the sea,
I am stag of seven combats,
I am a hawk upon a cliff,
I am a tear-drop of the sun,
I am fair,
I am a boar for valour,
I am a salmon in a pool,
I am a lake in a plain,
I am the excellence of arts,
I am a spear that wages battle with plunder,
I am a god who forms subjects for a ruler,
Who explains the stones of the mountains?
Who invokes the ages of the moon?
Where lies the setting of the sun?
Who bears cattle from the house of Tethra?
Who are the cattle of Tethra who laugh?
What man, what god forms weapons?
Indeed, then: I invoked a satirist...
A satirist of wind.

The Song of Amergin, translation by John Carey. The Celtic Heroic Age: Literary Sources for Ancient Celtic Europe and Early Ireland and Wales, by John T. Koch and John Carey, 1st edition, page 256-7.

The song of Amergin is an invocation that inspires me. On hearing these words, a magic awakens my soul. These ancient words were spoken by Amairgen Glanglun, a chief druid for the Milesians who lived in Ireland many moons ago. Amergin invoked these magical words to calm a wind, and quiet the ocean, which then allowed the Milesians to go on and defeat the Tuatha De Danann. It whispers a timeless essence about the interconnectedness of the natural world, and the power of the spoken word. This ancient song sees everything entwined in the great mystery of life. It represents how powerful language can be. *Am gaeth i m-muir.* I am a wind in the sea. This song reminds me that nature is my teacher, my healer, my kindred. Nature is a part of my soul, and that radiance that is within nature is also within all of us.

This book belongs to the fayeries – it is theirs, and yours to share. I have written about what I discovered from connecting to the subtle energies of nature; words from my inner knowing and perspective, and now you must find your own words to express the beauty of nature, of what you see beyond the veil, it is time to write your own fayerie tales, as those visions, and imaginings will be unique to you. In Ireland, there is an ancient saying that there are three truths – there is my truth, your truth, and the truth; and I keep this in mind, as our individuality is sacred.

In my search for a truth that resonated with my soul, a sincerity spoke to me in many places. Truth grounds me as I bask beneath the essence of a majestic tree. Truth radiates from my heart as I gaze into an animal's eyes, feeling them speak to my soul in a way only love can comprehend. Truth embodies me as the wind chills my face, or as the sun beams down on my being. Truth echoes between your and my heart, as in the stillness of silence we peer into each other's eyes, searching for words to express the beauty of nature. But we cannot find the words. I found this "essence of truth" and the light of God in all things. The great mystery shone forth from the light. We find that light in our own unique ways.

During the midst of my heart's awakening, I sat closer to the earth, nearer to the flowers and abundant hedgerows. I would catch moments of gentle peace when in contemplative prayer. This peace allowed me to hear the birds sing with no other interruption. The beauty in the natural landscapes can never be stolen. The gift of simplicity is rich indeed. The Elven one's whisper words of wisdom in simplicity; on the landscapes, on the breeze, in the evergreens.

As each heart opens, it becomes fine-tuned to the world, and as we connect to the Elven ones' song, we sense the gentle whispers of ancient fayerie in the animal, plant, and mineral kingdoms. And although we may never fully comprehend the magnitude of the fayerie worlds, we can admire the Otherworld's wisdoms from a distance.

Inside of us is a magical kingdom waiting to be explored. A kingdom that has forests and glens that need understanding, skies of inspiration that need exploring, and rivers of tears that need releasing.

It takes courage to transform and become whole beings as we awaken to our heart's knowing. As this vulnerable earth transforms, we are changing and ascending with her. The Elven ones are here to assist our journey, offering us a helping hand by enlightening our individual spirits, by igniting our sense of connection with the earth, where we weave our own stories about how we see the earth, in all its delicate beauty – just as our ancestors created stories of the fayerie realms. As we recognize the essence within the Elven ones, we kindle a light in our hearts. As we unlock our imaginations and vision to the "hidden" kingdoms, we unite with a higher spiritual consciousness that is within us.

What is invaluable is how we see this majestic earth. Connecting to the ancient fayerie is another way of seeing the beauty in our world, as it captivates our hearts. The fayerie stays "hidden" and rely on us to do our part in life.

Nature will be here long after we transcend to the Summerland's; her intelligence is infinite, authentic, and knowing. A belief in the fayerie world helps us to embody a gentleness towards the land, and that encourages us to take care of it. After all, is that not the fayeries' purpose all along. Maybe, the ancient myths and legends were spoken of to warn humans that their wrongdoings of destroying the natural environments will be met with adversity. Nature is our greatest ally, and the stories of ancient fayerie are here to remind us of that.

As we nurture our relationship with the earth and access our subconscious minds by connecting with the ancient fayerie, we are shown pathways into healing our heart's essence, and we reinstate our sense of belonging to this world. It is not the easiest of paths, to heal the holes inside of ourselves, delving into the underworld of our emotions, but it is necessary if we are to survive, and thrive new beginnings on earth, as she naturally transforms, and resets herself, as she moves into a new aeon.

May your search for your individual truth and meeting with the fayerie kingdoms lead you to a homecoming within your heart. May you be inspired by the wisdoms of the earth, and the People of Peace, and learn how to walk alongside this fragile planet, recognizing the common thread of unity in all our hearts.

The ancient fayerie await.

Bibliography and Further Reading

Ancient Legends of Ireland by Lady Wilde

An Carow Gwyn: Sorcery and the Ancient Fayerie Faith by Robin Artisson

Coming Home to the Trees by Patrick Jasper Lee

Cornish Folk-lore by Robert Hunt

Dealings with the Fairies by George MacDonald

Early British Trackways by Alfred Watkins

Encounters with Pan and the Elemental Kingdom by Robert Ogilvie Crombie

Fairy and Folk Tales of the Irish Peasantry by William Butler Yeats

From Granite to Sea: The folklore of Bodmin Moore and East Cornwall by Alex Langstone

Hands of Light by Barbara Brennan

Lebor Gabala Erenn, translated by Robert Macalister

Luna Moon Hare: A Magical Journey with the Goddess by Wendy Andrew

Meeting the Other Crowd: The Fairy Stories of Hidden Ireland by Carloyn Eve Green and Eddie Lenihan

North Cornwall Fairies and Legends by Enys Tregarthen

Preseli Bluestone: Healing Stone of the Ancestors by Simon and Sue Lilly

Primitive Culture by Edward Burnett Tyler

Scottish Fairy and Folk Tales by George Douglas

Silver Wheel: The Lost Teachings of the Deerskin Book by Elen Tompkins

The Andrew Lang Fairy Tale Treasury, edited by Cary Wilkins

The Book of Stones by Naisha Ahsian and Robert Simmons

The Book of the Flower Fairies by Cicely Mary Barker

The Boy Who Saw True, editor, Cyril Scott

The Celtic Heroic Age by John Koch and John Carey

The Celtic Twilight by William Butler Yeats

The Dragon's Edge by Peter Royston Smith

The Druid Plant Oracle by Philip and Stephanie Carr-Gomm

The Fairy Faith in Celtic Countries by Walter Evans-Wentz

The Mabinogion, early Welsh literature from a 14th century manuscript

The Middle Kingdom by Dermot Mac Manus

The Shamanic Journey: A Practical Guide to Therapeutic Shamanism by Paul Francis

The Sidhe by John Matthews

The Sun and the Serpent by Paul Broadhurst and Hamish Miller

The Vanishing People by Katharine Briggs

Acknowledgements

This book is a homage to the sacred guardians of the earth, the ancient fayerie, the Elven, the dragons, the dryads, the gnomes, the merfolk, for without their wisdoms, none of this would have been possible. I honour the light in them all.

I wish to thank – my family for nurturing my spiritual journey. Mum, for your unwavering faith; Dad, for showing me the beauty in nature; my big brother, for being you. Clarissa White and Claire Monk, for your endless encouragement. Wendy Winstanley, for being *Ancient Fayeries* guardian. Armorel Hamilton, for your shining fayerie inspiration. Pete Smith, for your steadfast wisdom. Eimear Burke, Elen Tompkins, and Wendy Andrews, for your heartfelt endorsements. I am grateful to my editor, Christine McPherson, and to Moon Books themselves. I am eternally thankful to Perpetua, Nana, and Grandad, who now rest in the Summerlands, I know you watched over me whilst I penned these words. And finally, I thank those who have inspired and encouraged me with their mentoring and teaching. I have learnt from many wise souls, and continue to do so along life's never-ending journey.

The Celtic wilderness is a consistent counsellor and mentor to us all. I am in awe of nature – the birds, the animals, the trees, rivers, mountains, and stones, who each share their voice. And I feel honoured to live by these Celtic shores which have transformed my mind, remedied my heart, and led to my homecoming.

Melanie

About the Author

Melanie Godfrey was born in Cheshire but grew up in Cornwall, the Land of Saints. Melanie has had a close affinity with nature and the spirit world since she was a child, often spending time in nature and believing it was made from pure magic. Melanie grew up seeing auras around people, and the unseen world of spirit. As her connection to spirit world developed, she began to see fayeries; they would appear from out of nowhere, within the home, in the woods, from behind a tree, in natural flourishing areas. From there, her love for the elemental world grew.

Melanie is an International Psychic Clairvoyant who has been working with the spirit world and subtle energies for the last twenty-six years, giving spiritual readings and healings to people from all over the world, and has worked extensively with animal communication and healing. Melanie is a qualified Therapeutic Counsellor with the Counselling and Psychotherapeutic Central Awarding Body UK, a Spiritualist Healer with The Healing Trust UK, and is currently studying Druidry with the Order of Bards, Ovates, and Druids.

MOON BOOKS

PAGANISM & SHAMANISM

What is Paganism? A religion, a spirituality, an alternative belief system, nature worship? You can find support for all these definitions (and many more) in dictionaries, encyclopaedias, and text books of religion, but subscribe to any one and the truth will evade you. Above all Paganism is a creative pursuit, an encounter with reality, an exploration of meaning and an expression of the soul. Druids, Heathens, Wiccans and others, all contribute their insights and literary riches to the Pagan tradition. Moon Books invites you to begin or to deepen your own encounter, right here, right now.

If you have enjoyed this book, why not tell other readers by posting a review on your preferred book site.

Recent bestsellers from Moon Books are:

Journey to the Dark Goddess
How to Return to Your Soul
Jane Meredith
Discover the powerful secrets of the Dark Goddess and
transform your depression, grief and pain into healing
and integration.
Paperback: 978-1-84694-677-6 ebook: 978-1-78099-223-5

Shamanic Reiki
Expanded Ways of Working with Universal Life Force Energy
Llyn Roberts, Robert Levy
Shamanism and Reiki are each powerful ways of healing; together,
their power multiplies. *Shamanic Reiki* introduces techniques to
help healers and Reiki practitioners tap ancient healing wisdom.
Paperback: 978-1-84694-037-8 ebook: 978-1-84694-650-9

Pagan Portals – The Awen Alone
Walking the Path of the Solitary Druid
Joanna van der Hoeven
An introductory guide for the solitary Druid, *The Awen Alone* will
accompany you as you explore, and seek out your own place
within the natural world.
Paperback: 978-1-78279-547-6 ebook: 978-1-78279-546-9

A Kitchen Witch's World of Magical Herbs & Plants
Rachel Patterson
A journey into the magical world of herbs and plants, filled with
magical uses, folklore, history and practical magic. By popular
writer, blogger and kitchen witch, Tansy Firedragon.
Paperback: 978-1-78279-621-3 ebook: 978-1-78279-620-6

Medicine for the Soul
The Complete Book of Shamanic Healing
Ross Heaven
All you will ever need to know about shamanic healing and how to
become your own shaman…
Paperback: 978-1-78099-419-2 ebook: 978-1-78099-420-8

Shaman Pathways – The Druid Shaman
Exploring the Celtic Otherworld
Danu Forest
A practical guide to Celtic shamanism with exercises and
techniques as well as traditional lore for exploring the Celtic
Otherworld.
Paperback: 978-1-78099-615-8 ebook: 978-1-78099-616-5

Traditional Witchcraft for the Woods and Forests
A Witch's Guide to the Woodland with Guided Meditations and
Pathworking
Mélusine Draco
A Witch's guide to walking alone in the woods, with guided
meditations and pathworking.
Paperback: 978-1-84694-803-9 ebook: 978-1-84694-804-6

Wild Earth, Wild Soul
A Manual for an Ecstatic Culture
Bill Pfeiffer
Imagine a nature-based culture so alive and so connected,
spreading like wildfire. This book is the first flame…
Paperback: 978-1-78099-187-0 ebook: 978-1-78099-188-7

Naming the Goddess
Trevor Greenfield
Naming the Goddess is written by over eighty adherents and
scholars of Goddess and Goddess Spirituality.
Paperback: 978-1-78279-476-9 ebook: 978-1-78279-475-2

Shapeshifting into Higher Consciousness
Heal and Transform Yourself and Our World with Ancient
Shamanic and Modern Methods
Llyn Roberts
Ancient and modern methods that you can use every day to
transform yourself and make a positive difference in the world.
Paperback: 978-1-84694-843-5 ebook: 978-1-84694-844-2

Readers of ebooks can buy or view any of these bestsellers by
clicking on the live link in the title. Most titles are published in
paperback and as an ebook. Paperbacks are available in traditional
bookshops. Both print and ebook formats are available online.

Find more titles and sign up to our readers' newsletter at
http://www.johnhuntpublishing.com/paganism
Follow us on Facebook at https://www.facebook.com/MoonBooks
and Twitter at https://twitter.com/MoonBooksJHP